The Sociological Quest

'*The Sociological Quest* provides an up-to-date, clear and comprehensive account of modern Sociology: where did it come from, what does it do, where is it going? Sociology often offers explanations of society and social change that are challenging and critical. In that context, Willis and Aarons invite students to join them on an exciting quest into what makes society tick and how we can best understand the social problems confronting individuals and societies. Through the sociological imagination, Sociologists address fundamental issues about what makes societies successful or unsuccessful'.

Bryan S. Turner, Professor of Sociology and Director of the Institute for Religion, Politics and Society at the Australian Catholic University, Australia, Honorary Professor and Director of the Centre for Citizenship, Social Pluralism and Religious Diversity at Potsdam University, Germany, and Emeritus Professor at the Graduate Center at the City University of New York City (CUNY), USA

Starting Sociology can be daunting. This user-friendly introduction takes the reader on a quest towards a sociological understanding of the world we live in. Using contemporary examples, *The Sociological Quest* asks what is distinctive about the way Sociologists view society. Haydn Aarons and Evan Willis show that they are concerned with the relationships between the individual and society, and that a sociological analysis involves an approach which is historical, cultural, structural, and critical.

This sixth edition has been thoroughly revised and updated and includes new material on identities, social change, social movements, populism, climate change, the COVID-19 pandemic, digital interaction, and social media. Also included in the sixth edition is an expanded chapter on empirical research in Sociology and the research process, as well as a new chapter on careers in Sociology.

Haydn Aarons is Senior Lecturer in Sociology at the Australian Catholic University in Melbourne, Australia. He has been teaching and researching in Sociology for over twenty years. He has published widely on a range of sociological topics including religion, health, rural communities, cultural consumption, and quantitative research methods.

Evan Willis is Adjunct Professor of Public Health at La Trobe University, Australia. He has had a long and distinguished career as a researcher and teacher in Sociology. His book, *Medical Dominance: The Division of Labour in Australian Health Care* (Routledge, 1989), was winner of the Australian Sociological Association Award in 2003 for the Ten Most Influential Books in Sociology.

The Sociological Quest

An Introduction to the Study of
Social Life

Sixth Edition

Haydn Aarons and Evan Willis

Routledge
Taylor & Francis Group

LONDON AND NEW YORK

Cover image: Getty Images

Sixth edition published 2023
by Routledge
4 Park Square, Milton Park, Abingdon, Oxon OX14 4RN

and by Routledge
605 Third Avenue, New York, NY 10158

Routledge is an imprint of the Taylor & Francis Group, an Informa business

© 2023 Haydn Aarons and Evan Willis

First edition published by Allen & Unwin 2011
Fifth edition published by Routledge 2020

British Library Cataloguing-in-Publication Data
A catalogue record for this book is available from the British Library

ISBN: 978-1-032-32708-2 (hbk)
ISBN: 978-1-032-32709-9 (pbk)
ISBN: 978-1-003-31632-9 (ebk)

DOI: 10.4324/9781003316329

Typeset in Bembo
by Newgen Publishing UK

To Claudia and Noah

Contents

Preface

This book is an introductory essay on the discipline of Sociology. It outlines to students, both those in the early stages of their studies, and those more generally interested in what Sociology has to offer, some of the important components of a sociological way of understanding the social world. With extensive use of examples, the book attempts to distil some of the key elements of sociological reasoning about the social world. The book arises out of having taught introductory Sociology at tertiary level, first tutoring and then lecturing, one of us (EW) for nearly five decades and the other for more than two decades (HA). It introduces students to a subject with which they are unlikely to be very familiar despite having been members of society for a long time. Yet the task of introducing students to this discipline is a challenging one. This book is not only an attempt to codify what we have taught over that time, but also reflects a belief in the need to introduce the discipline pedagogically in a particular manner. The analogy often used is that getting into Sociology is like getting into a swimming pool that has no shallow end. The aim with introductory courses in the subject, as with this book, is not to construct an artificial shallow end, such that the students have to learn later that it's not all as simple as that, but rather to provide something by way of a buoyancy vest. This will get them into the discipline in a way where they won't drown, but neither will they get an unrealistic idea of how straightforward it all is either. The central tenets of the discipline are presented in a manner which attempts to be both straightforward and understandable without either doing too much damage to the complexity of the issues, or greatly affecting the readability of the book, with continual qualification of statements being made. The balance between making the discipline both interesting and understandable on one hand, while at the same time not oversimplifying unduly is a considerable balancing act. This book represents our attempt, on the basis of long experience and much feedback in many universities in different countries to achieve this aim.

New editions have been prepared in response to two needs. One is the helpful comments from many of the users, especially tutors in the subjects in which this book has been used, as to how the book could be made more useful for the purposes of introducing students to the discipline of Sociology. The other is the need to keep the illustrative examples current and contemporary. Over time, it has also become apparent that introductory Sociology subjects are not the only area where this book has proved useful. The other is service courses on Sociology in professional and multidisciplinary postgraduate degrees. Examples have been added on the basis of ongoing feedback from students and instructors using the book. Once again though, we have attempted to impart a fairly traditional view of the discipline of Sociology, in terms of which, and subsequently against which instructors can teach in subsequent years if they so choose. Finally, a note to instructors. In its earlier editions, which include an international edition (Rutgers University Press, New Jersey, 1996), as well as a Norwegian edition (with Aksel Tjora, *Pa Sociologisk Spor: En innforing I sociologisk fortaelse*. Tapir Academisk Forlag, Trondheim, Norway, 2006), this book has proved most useful as a supplement to an established textbook of introductory Sociology, to be used in the first four to six weeks of an introductory subject as a means of stimulating the sociological imagination. It attempts to whet students' appetite for the task of studying the discipline which lies ahead. The book has also proved particularly useful for students studying in multidisciplinary settings to access an introduction to a sociological style of reasoning.

1   Introduction

A number of today's video games involve a quest (quest: a search or pursuit made in order to find or obtain something. *The Macquarie Dictionary*). In these carefully written programs the designer takes the players on a journey, often challenging and difficult, in order to achieve something at the end. In their search or pursuit, the players must gather various tools to assist them, making the task easier by helping them overcome the obstacles that lie in their path.

Think of this short book as educational software designed to lead students on a quest to understand the social world and how it is changing. It is not an easy quest; it is likely to be a challenge that at times will be frustrating. But ultimately it is designed not only to be enjoyable but also to be a useful part of what it means to be educated, either for its own sake or as part of a programme of study leading to professional qualifications. Along the path to sociological understanding, tools are available to assist in the quest. These tools are sociological ones in the form of concepts. As we shall see, when these concepts are woven into sociological theories and methods, they help us make sense of social life.

The origins of Sociology

The term 'Sociology', an amalgam of Latin and Greek meaning 'reasoning about the social', was coined by the Frenchman Auguste Comte in 1842. The discipline has emerged and gained coherence in the many years since Comte gave it its name, first in

DOI: 10.4324/9781003316329-1

Europe and then progressively in North America and many other parts of the world. Sociological thinking, in the guise of social philosophy, however, has been with us for many centuries. Plato's *The Republic*, for example, considers important questions about the ideal state and its structure through social relations. Parallel forms of enquiry to Sociology can also be discerned from individuals based in centres of learning outside of Europe, such as the medieval Arabic philosopher Ibn Khaldun (Dhaouadi: 1990) and Chinese philosopher Confucius.

The 'twin' revolutions of late eighteenth-century Europe – the French and Industrial Revolutions – provided the context in which Sociology emerged. During the French Revolution (beginning in 1789), the masses overthrew the aristocracy and brought about the end of monarchical rule. The process began earlier in the century in the period known as the Enlightenment, during which laws based on religious principles were gradually challenged in favour of those based on more secular, rational thought. The Industrial Revolution of the eighteenth and nineteenth centuries transformed the British economy from being agriculturally based to factory based.

Sociology as a discipline came into being in Europe as an attempt to understand and make sense of these massive changes. All aspects of European society were affected by these profound philosophical, economic, and political changes. Family, work, transportation, entertainment, and medicine were all dramatically changed as a result of these overlapping historical events, which became associated with the development of what we now call *modernity*, used here in the sense of post-Enlightenment social processes.

The early Sociologists struggled to analyse and come to terms with the meaning of these social changes. Indeed the Social Sciences in general and Sociology in particular came into being as a direct response to the social problems of modernity, as Harriss (2000: 325) has argued. The early Sociologists asked a number of questions, including, 'Why have these changes occurred?' and, 'What has been the impact of all these changes on our society and the way people live their lives?' The questions they asked and the answers they sought set much of the agenda for the sociological investigation that, to a greater or lesser extent, is still being worked upon today. Such an approach has come into stark definition as we embark on the process of making sense of the massive changes on a world scale, to all these areas of society and the economy associated with the emergence in 2020 of the Coronavirus pandemic. More on this later. Furthermore, the efforts of the early Sociologists contributed to the impact of those changes. What distinguished their efforts was the way they posed questions about what was happening to the societies in which they lived. We refer to these questions as their sense of *sociological problem*.

The French Revolution had profound effects in the overturning of an existing social order by a social movement based on the *secular* (that is, non-religious) principles of universal liberty and equality. Although geographically limited to France, its impact was felt throughout the world as a climate of political change was created, a change to which many societies responded and are continuing to respond. This fundamental change in the distribution of power was prompted by the emergence of democracy, a dynamic force that has become a symbol of political transformation, the effects of which are still being felt in many diverse societies.

The Industrial Revolution began in Britain in the eighteenth century and spread to Europe and the United States in the nineteenth century. It is associated with the emergence of industry and the transition of social, economic, and political arrangements over a substantial period of time, which altered the way the various groups in society related to each other. The revolution therefore consisted of two related aspects: technological and social. The harnessing of steam power and the development of manufacturing and factories brought massive social and economic changes, including urbanisation and the growth of cities, as the capitalist system of production developed and replaced feudalism as the basis of the social order.

The extent of the changes in the established social order was apparent to a number of writers and thinkers from a variety of backgrounds. Each in their own way attempted to make sense of the changes occurring around them at that time. These changes were not only economic, they were also profoundly political and moral in character. The meaning and implications of these changes for how societies functioned were the subject of detailed analyses of the emergence of what we now call the modern world. For the majority of Sociologists, the most important of these analyses were by three seminal figures: Emile Durkheim, Karl Marx, and Max Weber. They each gave different answers to the sociological problem of what was happening to the world as they knew it. Most of their answers were critical, and each was different and distinctive. These diverse threads of explanation came to be called Sociology.

For Karl Marx (1818–83), the transformation was understood primarily as a change in the *economic structure* of societies – a change in the means by which economic production was organised from a system called feudalism to one called capitalism. Other massive changes, he believed, flowed from this change in the economic or *material conditions* under which people lived. Marx's contribution was not only to Sociology; the effect of his ideas on the modern world through politics, economics, and philosophy has been enormous given the role his ideas have played in alternative systems of economic production to capitalism.

While Marx was trying to provide the intellectual and political basis for the change in the social order, the issue for Frenchman Emile Durkheim (pronounced 'Derk-hime'), who lived from 1858 to 1917, was more of how to preserve it. According to Durkheim the basis for social order (how society hung together and worked over time) was not economic but moral, expressed in the type of solidarity that a society exhibited. Prior to the great changes brought about by the twin revolutions leading to modernity, social order had been based on what he called *mechanical solidarity* – people belonged on the basis of a smaller, less socially differentiated society, where everyone performed similar activities. Integration was possible because of shared assumptions and lifestyles. These shared assumptions tended to promote a common morality. The massive transformation in society associated with the advent of modernity could be analysed as a move towards *organic solidarity*, where integration occurs on the basis of special-isation of work tasks, on dependence upon each other to meet human needs through a *division of labour*. Societies had to actively promote a strong sense of shared morality, he believed, in order to overcome the potentially harmful consequences of modern-isation – a process he felt distinctively ambivalent about due to its tendency to produce *anomie*, that is, a feeling of being uprooted and morally displaced due to change.

The German Max Weber (pronounced 'Vey-ber') lived from 1864 to 1920, and he, too, was distinctly ambivalent about the changes occurring in society. He studied other societies, such as India and China, which had not undergone such monumental changes, in order to understand the distinctiveness of the modern Western world. For Weber, the key change was in the growth of *rationality*, that of basing decisions not on tradition or other considerations but on what is considered the best and most effi-cient means of reaching a particular goal. The growth of ration-ality had been occurring over several centuries in the Western world and according to Weber it was particularly manifested in the changing basis for authority. His theory of social change was that gradually *legal–rational authority*, where leadership is based on legally endorsed formal rules such as the election of a prime minister, had gradually replaced either *traditional authority* (such as a monarchy, where authority stems from family membership over several generations) or *charismatic authority* (based on extra-ordinary personal characteristics of the leader).

Other social theorists also sought to understand the changes, but Marx, Durkheim, and Weber are considered the most important from the perspective of modern Sociology. They agreed that something major had happened to the European society they lived in, but disagreed on what exactly had taken place, why change had occurred, and what the consequences were. The basis for their analyses rested upon different assumptions or prem-ises and ultimately upon different theoretical foundations. These will be explored in more detail later in this book because they still provide much of the core agenda at the foundation of the concerns of the discipline. The unique manner in which they took aspects of society as sociological problems has become the hallmark of a sociological perspective.

What's to come?

The path of this particular quest for sociological understanding of the social world has not been an easy one, as the monumental changes to society leading to modernity and beyond are highly complex. Sociology has grown to be one of the most popular tertiary subjects for study, with its practitioners contributing at every level of society to improve our understanding of what is happening to the social world as we know it. However, Sociology retains a somewhat controversial character. All members of society obviously have experience in understanding and analysing what is going on around them. What Sociologists do is sometimes assumed to be mainly the analysis of commonsense dressed up in fancy language or jargon that is difficult for others to understand. Furthermore, what Sociologists have had to say about how our society works has sometimes offended those with vested interests in society and has, on occasion, been uncomfortable for those who benefit most from the current social organisation of society, such as those with a dominant ethnicity or gender, or who have great wealth and opportunity.

It is difficult not to be interested in what is happening to our own society and to the social world in which we live. We are all fundamentally social animals; that is to say, we behave socially in the sense that our behaviour is shaped by the expectations and responses of others. As individuals, we are immersed in what we call *social processes*, which make up social life. At the same time we are also members of various groups, hence the focus on *social interaction*, or how people relate to one another. It is social interaction between various groups that is the primary focus of Sociology. These might be small-scale groups of only a few individuals such as families, medium-scale groups such as workplaces or schools, or large-scale groups such as nation states. Interaction between individuals in these groups can be understood as occurring in regular, systematic patterns over time. A number of different academic (social science) disciplines take this broad issue of the relationship between the individual and the group as their subject matter, such as economics, politics, and anthropology, but Sociology is the one that focuses most centrally upon it.

The aim of this short book is to launch the reader on a 'sociological quest' for understanding the social world. At its most basic, it is argued that Sociology is a 'way of seeing' the world. Adopting a sociological viewpoint is akin to putting on a pair of spectacles. It enables the wearer not only to see better but also brings certain aspects into clearer focus. An alternative pair of spectacles (by analogy say a psychological one, for example) will give another way of seeing and bring other aspects into perspective. For example, the great changes to European society heralding modernity that were mentioned earlier have been interpreted in numerous atomised ways as a series of intellectual, political, or economic changes, but a sociological perspective on these events brings a unique view to them that enables us to attempt questions about how society changes overall and establishes how social processes and social relationships are also changed as a result. More on this in a later chapter.

So this book considers how sociological explanations differ from those provided by other academic scholarly disciplines. The argument is that Sociology has a particular concern with the relationship between the individual and society, which makes it distinct from other sorts of social explanation. In subsequent chapters, this theme is explored in some detail through the idea of the *sociological imagination*, a concept devised by the American sociologist C. Wright Mills.

Applying the sociological imagination to the understanding of any social phenomenon involves considering four distinct elements or components: historical, cultural, structural, and critical. Much of this book is devoted to explaining and illustrating how these aspects are central to the quest of understanding the social world in sociological terms. Later in the book we consider the issues of sociological perspectives and their relationship to methods of gathering information about the world. Finally, we will look at some of the process issues of 'doing Sociology' and how Sociology can lead to a rewarding career.

References

Dhaouadi, M., 1990. 'Ibn Khaldun: The Founding Father of Eastern Sociology', *International Sociology*, 5, 319–335.

Harriss, J., 2000. 'The Second Great Transformation? Capitalism at the End of the Twentieth Century'. In Allen, T., and Thomas, A. (eds), *Poverty and Development into the 21st Century*, revised edn, Oxford University Press, Oxford: 325–342.

2 The nature of sociological explanation

In this chapter, some of the fundamental aspects of the socio-logical explanation are considered. These are the distinction between sociological and social problems; the question of private troubles and public issues; the distinction between the macro, large-scale level of analysis and the micro, small-scale level; the issue of reflexivity as well as issues of continuity and change.

Sociological and social problems

What sorts of things are Sociologists interested in? Generally speaking they are interested in all aspects of the social world – why is it like it is? These are sociological problems. They are not the same as social problems, however, and understanding the difference between the two is important when embarking on the sociological quest.

A *sociological problem* is that which demands explanation. It is usually cast in the form of a question inciting intellectual curiosity. It is a problem in the sense that it needs to be understood and explained. Each of the early Sociologists took as their sense of sociological problem the question of, 'What is happening to our society as we know it?' A *social problem*, by contrast, is an aspect of the organisation of society that someone thinks needs to be addressed and solved.

Sociological and social problems sometimes coincide, but they may also consider different aspects of the phenomenon in question. Some examples will make this point clearer. Take the

DOI: 10.4324/9781003316329-2

COVID-19 pandemic. The massive death toll across the world prior to the vaccines becoming broadly effective and reducing that toll is clearly a social problem in terms of the implications for family, work life, and travel, amongst many other consequences. A sociological problem, however, may be to consider what it is about the way our society is organised that the impact has not been felt uniformly across high-income and low-income nations on the one hand, and then within different societies by social class, racial background, and gender on the other.

Another example is unemployment. We can probably agree that it is a social problem, that there is not enough paid work for all those who want it. A sociological problem, however, may be to consider what it is about the way our society is organised that it does not provide enough paid work opportunities. Alternatively, we might consider why those without work have difficulty maintaining a sense of worth – is it because a person's identity (their sense of who they are and where they fit in the world) comes from the sort of job they perform?

Another example relates to a tragic case in Norway in 2021 where the body of an Oslo man was discovered an estimated nine years after he died (*Guardian* 2021). Everyone involved was dismayed at how few friends or acquaintances the man had even in a highly connected society like Norway. He was reported to have been married at least once and had several children. In the United Kingdom, even during a period of heightened social surveillance during the COIVID 19 pandemic 'people have died at home alone and not been found for up to two weeks, doctors who have investigated such deaths have said. They have only been discovered after a relative, friend or neighbour raised the alarm and have in many cases gone undetected for so long that their body has started to decompose' (Campbell 2020).

But from a sociological point of view the broader issue is also about growing urban isolation or what might broadly be called an epidemic of loneliness. Sociologists use the term *social networks* to analyse how many relationships with other people individuals have. The trend seems to be towards people being less connected with society and more alone, despite the growth and extent of social media use (O'Day and Heimberg 2021), especially those with fewer economic resources. The issue is clearly an important one in planning future cities.

A sociological problem may not necessarily be a social problem. Sociological problems can be found at all levels of the social world – at the individual, community, societal, or global levels. Reading the morning newspaper is likely to stimulate curiosity about all sorts of sociological problems. Some have serious implications, some not. A number of examples at different levels will make this clearer.

At the *individual* level, take the opportunity the next time you travel in a lift to observe where other people stand after entering. Is there a pattern in the way that the physical space is progressively occupied? The pattern you will most likely observe (not always, but often enough to make it a recurring feature of social life) is as follows. When the first person has taken up a position at the lift controls, the next will stand in the opposite diagonal corner. The next two who enter will fill the other corners and those that follow will stand in the spaces in between. The unconscious understanding of these patterns is widely shared by the community, such that if it is deliberately flouted, for instance, by standing right next to the only other person in the lift, it is likely that they would feel threatened and may exit at the first possible opportunity!

This is not a social problem in the sense of something that needs addressing but it is a sociological problem in the sense of being curious. How lifts are occupied happens in a predictable manner that is curious. Why do people act in this way? The usual explanation given is in terms of maximising personal space. The lift is occupied in such a manner as to retain as much space between strangers as possible. Similar patterns of 'colonisation' of public space happen in other settings such as cafeterias and on public transport.

In a famous essay in the social sciences, called 'The Stranger' (1959), German sociologist Georg Simmel posed a sociological problem or question, 'What is it about the quality of being a stranger to a social setting that prompts certain patterns of behaviour?' Consider the situation of being told a life story by someone you have never met before and whom you happen to be sitting beside on a long plane or rail journey. This example of what Simmel called a 'sociological form' is nicely captured in the 1988 movie *The Accidental Tourist* about a travel writer who advises readers on how to avoid others while travelling but is besieged by the person next to him on a plane, who proceeds to tell him their life story. It is not a social problem in the sense of it being an aspect of our society that needs fixing. But it is a sociological problem since it provokes thought and more questions about the phenomenon. It happens often enough to be obvious that more of an explanation is needed than just understanding the personality of the 'stranger'. What is it about long journeys that invites strangers to reveal intimate details of their lives to each other? Why do we feel compelled to listen? Are men more likely to reveal details of their lives to other men or to women (and vice versa)?

Instead, it is a sociological problem at a fundamental level; it is curious what explains this behaviour and this can be a starting point for conducting research in an attempt to answer the question. Perhaps it is the journey itself, providing an opportunity for reflection, that an individual then feels like sharing their life with the person sitting near them. Perhaps it is the expectation that they will never again encounter the person which releases them from the usual constraints on revealing aspects of their personal life to others.

Another example of the stranger concerns patterns of social interaction on social media sites such as Twitter where the phenomenon of 'sliding into someone's DM's' (direct messages) or certain responses to posts from 'reply guys' have become an issue. Let's say you tweet an opinion on one single occasion. Then someone propositions you via a direct message, or responds to your tweet publicly in a way that isn't solicited, invited, or acceptable to you. Similarly, with the massive reach and accessibility of social media, there is the onset and devastation of the 'pile on' where not just one stranger comments on a post, but potentially hundreds of thousands of strangers fume vitriol on a person online because of a post (Ronson 2016). What is it about social media that seems to make people feel freer to engage in such ways that we would have to assume they would not otherwise?

Certainly, a lot of social media is public and replies to posts are to be expected, yet the etiquette to responding is still being worked out. However, socially defined parameters that acknowledge the harm and problematic consequences of online abuse are emerging. The online abuse of women and cyber-bullying are two key areas of concern here.

From the examples above, Sociologists would pose a number of questions about the nature of social interaction between individuals that is governed by common or shared values, and how certain kinds of interaction breach or compromise these values. Is there some kind of bravado in hiding behind an anonymous social media profile that uproots regular forms of social interaction? Do travelers on public modes of transport feel that it is an open social space so as to share their stories with anyone else within earshot?

Sociological problems at the *community* level are a little broader. Many community-level sociological problems involve considering why some people behave differently from others. Elections and referenda are ostensibly political events but those elected to or dismissed from public office, or what decisions a citizenry make via popular vote, are often related to various social patterns heavily influencing how communities react at the ballot box. In recent history one particular election and a referendum stand as fascinating sociological phenomena in and of themselves. Few pundits tipped Donald Trump to win the 2016 US presidential election. Similarly, the outcome of the vote to withdraw the United Kingdom from the European Union ('Brexit') was unexpected. The aftermath of both results left scholars scrambling for explanations, and what emerged as was a roll call of key sociological patterns highlighting various community faultlines. These included: perceived urban elites vs 'forgotten' white working-class American and British communities, polarised and segregated communities of rich and poor and of black, people of colour, and white, and highly educated cosmopolitan bubbles versus ordinary people in the 'heartlands'. What has emerged, in the United States especially, is a citizenry that deeply mistrusts the political process, is more violent, and more divided. This has happened to the extent that, inconceivably, around three hundred

Trump supporters violently stormed the Capitol Building to disrupt the Congress from formalising Joe Biden as president.

Another example of a social problem at the community level is the reaction to mask and vaccine mandates aimed at reducing the infection rates of COVID-19. While in many countries a majority of people have complied with government regulations and health advice to get vaccinated and wear a mask, especially indoors in public places, a significant minority are refusing. Such civil disobedience has been augmented with public protests, demonstrations, and online posturing to create a protest movement. Further, some people even forwent their employment in industries such as teaching and nursing by refusing vaccination rather than conform to government or employer requirements.

Understanding and explaining the sociological problem of what the victories of Donald Trump and Brexit mean is essential before the other side of the question can be considered. The social problem associated with this phenomenon is, 'How do countries like the United States keep democratic norms in place and ensure fair representation in politics?' The social and sociological problems in this example are related but focus on different aspects. The sociological focus is, 'Why is it so?' as well as 'What can be done about it?' For the anti-vaxxers and anti-maskers the social problems are to do with the severe health risks they posed for themselves and others. But the sociological problem here is whether there is a pattern to people who are anti-vaccination and why these people felt so strongly about it?

An example of a sociological problem at a *societal* level could look at unemployment and underemployment (that is people working less hours than they would choose to). In the process of *globalisation*, as barriers to trade are gradually removed and individual nation states and their industries increasingly attempt to be competitive on a global scale, the task of finding adequate employment for all members of a society who want it, is a major one for legislators. The sociological problem may be to consider what it is about the way our society is currently organised that it does not provide enough paid work opportunities, particularly for groups such as women and recently arrived persons to places such as Australia. Employment leading to economic prosperity has been curtailed for these groups due to historic gender roles as mothers and home makers and other forms of systematic exclusion such as sexism and racism. If people are having to work longer hours to keep their jobs, could this extra work not be shared around so more people who are looking for work can do some of it?

We might consider the question posed earlier about how work is bound up with a person's sense of worth. When two people meet, one of the most important ways in which they locate each other in the social world ('Who are you?') is by asking what sort of work they do. The sociological question would be, 'Why is this so?' Might it be better to promote social identity through people's leisure interests – 'I'm a chess player who just happens to earn a living as a motor mechanic'?

Within particular societies, Sociologists focus on aspects of how those societies are organised. An example is conflict on the basis of race or ethnicity in many different countries. Race has been a strong focus for Sociologists in recent years with the rise of social movements such as Black Lives Matter in the United States and Aboriginal Lives Matter in Australia. There is a historical legacy of slavery, oppression, exclusion, and segregation of black Americans in the United States. The sociological question, clearly needing a historical perspective is, why do black Americans continue to experience forms of state-sanctioned brutality and exclusion? Similarly, why are First Nations peoples of colonised countries such as Australia, New Zealand, Canada, and the United States, still precarious and marginalised citizens in those respective societies?

Sociological problems at a *global* or macro level are also grist to the Sociologists' mill. Will our social world experience fundamental changes as a result of the Coronavirus pandemic? Now that the evidence for climate change in the direction of global warming appears incontrovertible, what shifts do we face in the ways humans live their lives? Likewise, how are rapid improvements in digital communication, artificial intelligence, and machine learning affecting the future of work and social interaction?

The sociological quest is concerned with the pursuit of explanations for sociological problems. It is the search for the general in the particular; that is, to consider individual experience as part of a pattern that may explain aspects of what is occurring in society as a whole. Sociologists routinely look for patterns in people's collective behaviour for explanation. An example might make this point clearer. In democratic societies, richer people generally vote conservative and poorer people vote for parties espousing more progressive political policies. However, there are some interesting counter patterns that have occurred, for instance some wealthier people voting for progressive parties such as the Greens, and some poorer people supporting conservative candidates and issues such as Trump and Brexit, which we discussed earlier. We say 'generally' because it doesn't always happen like that but enough that there is a pattern to be explained. At the risk of overgeneralising, richer people want to conserve their social position in society, while poorer people prefer political parties that, notionally at least, have policies that ameliorate social inequality and improve their lot.

From these examples it can be seen that Sociology can operate at a number of levels: from micro, to meso, to macro. Micro Sociology is concerned with what happens in small social groups. Meso Sociology is concerned with middle-level questions such as those within communities. Macro Sociology is more concerned with the broader context of large groups, including whole societies. Sociology can consider individual-level problems such as the quality of being a stranger; community-level issues such as social division; national-level questions such as national identity; and global-level questions such as migration or the integration of economies. At their most basic level, posing questions of a sociological nature is likely to stimulate curiosity of the most fundamental, 'Why is it so?' variety. Sociological and social problems, furthermore, are obviously related to one another; understanding the phenomenon in question (the sociological problem) is an essential precursor to doing something about it (trying to solve the social problem).

The sociological imagination

Sociology may be considered a particular means of approaching, understanding and explaining collective human behaviour. Different writers have characterised this most basic insight slightly differently. For Peter Berger (1963), the sociological quest is for a form of consciousness which fosters examination of the social world and results in a better understanding of it. For John Goldthorpe (2016) the sociological quest is a population science that discerns key broad patterns of continuity and change in social action. For C. Wright Mills (1959), the quest is for what he called the sociological imagination. Such an imagination focuses on the place of the individual in the larger scheme of things: the relationship between the individual and society, between the biography of individual members of any particular society and the broad history of that particular society. A key distinction characteristic of the sociological imagination is that between *personal troubles* and *public issues*. This distinction, Wright Mills (1959: 14) argues, 'is an essential tool of the sociological imagination and a feature of all classic work in social science'.

Personal troubles happen to individuals, they may be a private matter in which cherished values are threatened. Public issues occur in the wider context and have to do with the way society, and particularly its social institutions, is organised into a social structure. Here some public value may be threatened. Let's consider some examples to illustrate the distinction between personal troubles and public issues.

When we ask in lectures for a show of hands of those students whose lives have been touched by youth suicide (that is, they know someone first hand who has taken their own life), many hands are raised. For young people, especially males, personal troubles don't come much bigger than an individual feeling that life has so little to offer them that they prefer the alternative. Yet there are also public issues of the type raised by sociologist Fran Baum (1998) in response to such a tragedy of private grief in her own family. These include:

- What are the social forces that have brought about a doubling of male suicide rates inside a quarter of a century?
- How can we restructure society to prevent this epidemic from worsening?

In the example above, these private troubles can be understood in terms of the 'place of the individual in the larger scheme of things'. Sociologists focus, not so much on the individual psychology of suicide but on factors like growing social isolation in urban contexts, the difficulty of making a clear transition to adulthood, especially for young males, and the precariousness of much of the work that young people are able to access, as well as changing gender roles.

Another example is injury and deaths at work. According to Safe Work Australia, three industries account for over half of work-related fatalities: transport, agriculture, and construction (Safe Work Australia 2019). Within these industries there are specific jobs that are over-represented in the fatality statistics, such as machine operators, drivers, and labourers; professionals in these industries have minimal injuries and deaths. That's a personal trouble. Yet, at an estimated cost to the Australian community of $61 billion each year (almost the same as the total health outlay by the Australian Government), with 77 per cent of that cost borne by workers themselves, workplace injury and death is also a public issue (Safe Work Australia 2019).

This issue concerns the organisation of work and cannot be explained simply in terms of worker carelessness or other individualistic explanations such as 'accidents'. The sociological imagination focuses attention on the social structure of the society in which we live to ask the question, 'What is it about the way things are organised in this society that is causing such loss of life?' Does the explanation lie in the way in which economic production is organised for profit, so that a tension or contradiction might be said to exist between safety and profit, for instance? How successful have attempts at regulation of workplaces been if workers are still being killed and injured in substantial numbers? What will be the implications of increasing deregulation of workplaces for worker health and safety? The changes to the system of awards under which Australians work that came into effect in July 1998 saw protective clothing, first-aid facilities, and some other occupational health and safety protections defined outside the new minimum award conditions.

Another example is gun ownership. In one of a number of tragic incidents which have occurred in the United States, a woman was accidentally shot dead by her two-year-old toddler son who reached into her handbag and found a handgun while shopping at a Walmart store in Idaho (*The Age* 2014). Her tragic death is a personal trouble, both for her friends and family, but it also raises a public issue about the role of firearms in American society. Unintentional firearm deaths in the United States, for instance, averaged 413 per year in the period 2005–15, the majority of them children and young people (Solnick and Hemenway 2019).

The COVID-19 pandemic has worsened this situation in the United States where there has been a collision of this public health crisis with that of gun violence. The onset of the pandemic saw a surge in gun purchases in 2020 resulting in an estimated 5.9 million guns sold from March to May 2020, an 80 per cent increase over the same time in 2019 (Everytown Research 2020). With all these extra guns in the home, and children not at school during the pandemic, there has been a spike in accidental shootings at home by children. Deadly unintentional shootings were up 43 per cent in March and April 2020, compared to the same months in the previous two years – an additional 354 deaths (Everytown Research 2020).

As Wright Mills (1959:15) argues, personal troubles become public issues when 'both the correct statement of the problem and the range of possible solutions require us to consider the political and economic institutions of the society and not merely the personal situation and character of a scatter of individuals'. This distinction is crucial to the quest for the sociological understanding of the relationship between the individual and society. Central to Sociology, then, is the attempt to understand the place of the individual in the larger scheme of things.

Other social science disciplines are also concerned with the relationship between the individual and society. It is not the exclusive preserve of the discipline of Sociology. The next chapter considers some of the differences between the disciplines, but for now the uniqueness of the discipline lies in the way explanation is sought in the way society is organised as a whole and the experience of individuals understood in that context. Another way to put this is that the concept of social structure acts as a sort of signpost to the questions to ask. As Coulson and Riddell (1970: 15) argue:

Our idea of what sociology is, what distinguishes it from other disciplines, lies in the way sociologists approach the explanation of phenomena as problems. They seek causes for them in *the fact of people's membership of social groups* and in the ways in which these groups are related to each other.

(Emphasis added)

Reflexivity

Seeking explanation for social phenomena in the way society is organised as a whole and in terms of the social groups to which people belong provides the framework for interpreting the experience of individuals, including ourselves. Important to the sociological quest, the pursuit of sociological imagination or consciousness, therefore, is the act of reflexivity. Being reflexive involves considering one's own place in the social world, not as an isolated and asocial individual but as a consequence of one's experience as a member of social groups. The experience of being a citizen of any nation therefore, will vary greatly according to whatever an individual's gender, ethnic background, age, sexual preference, and class happens to be. A couple of examples may make this point clearer.

In difficult economic times, when jobs are scarce, especially for school leavers, an understandable response by young people has been to attempt to improve their chances in the job market by securing higher levels of qualifications. At the very least, staying out of the job market for a few more years while tertiary qualifications are gained (what has been called 'warehousing the young') may see employment prospects improve by the time these qualifications are gained. The consequences of large numbers of individuals seeking to improve their qualifications has been twofold. There has been an increased demand for places in the tertiary education system, and there has been 'inflation' in the qualifications needed to enter many careers. Jobs that were once done by high school graduates now require a university degree as the point of entry. The sociological term for this process is *credentialism*.

The outcome has been great disappointment, dashed hopes, and reorientation to new careers on the part of the (mainly) young people concerned. Reflexivity on the part of these young people reveals the fact that their membership of the social group – school leavers at that particular time – was obviously crucial to understanding the whole set of events. A sense of perspective on how the labour market changes and what the implications are for young people seeking to enter that labour market is essential. Focusing only at the individual level on individual failings is of limited usefulness. Entering the labour market by getting a job is like a race in which the finishing line keeps being moved.

Another example is the occupational health and safety issue discussed above. Seeking cause in 'the fact of people's membership of social groups' directs attention to examining those areas of the workforce where most fatalities occur. In this case, it is the areas of the workforce where production occurs, such as driving a vehicle or operating a machine. It is the bottom rungs of the workforce which are overwhelmingly represented amongst fatalities. Not too many fatalities or indeed occupational injuries are reported from boardrooms!

A further example is the consequences of 'natural' disasters related to a changing global climate. Hurricane Katrina wreaked havoc on the US city of New Orleans in August 2005 with more than 1,800 deaths. The devastating toll of human life and homelessness fell not on the wealthy, who were able to leap in their SUV vehicles and escape to higher ground, but overwhelmingly on the poor black working-class communities (see Elliott and Andais 2006).

So, the sociological quest is not only an intellectual one but one in which individual seekers are likely to reflexively develop a better understanding of their society and of their place in it. So much of the social world we tend to take for granted; what Sociology can offer, as Waters and Crook (1990: 27) argue, is 'a different sort of vision on a familiar world'. Putting on our sociological spectacles brings certain aspects of reality into closer focus. The sociological quest invites us:

> to look at our familiar surroundings as if for the first time. It allows us to get a fresh view of the world we have always taken for granted, to examine our own social landscape with the same curiosity and fascination that we might bring to an

exotic, alien culture ... Sociology also gives us a window on the wider world that lies beyond our immediate experience leading us into areas of society we might otherwise have ignored or misunderstood.

(Robertson 1987: 4)

Continuity and change

As these examples show, contemporary Sociologists are still grappling with and trying to make sense of the set of core issues developed and given coherence by earlier Sociologists. Sociology has evolved a long way since those days and the study of society has developed in a number of directions, but many Sociologists (ourselves included) believe the issues they were interested in still have relevance today. There is the problem of social order or continuity on the one hand, and the problem of change on the other. How is it that despite our unique and individual experiences and backgrounds, our idiosyncrasies and individual foibles, we manage as a society to exist and survive over time? How is it that if you were to leave your country tomorrow for five years, when you return it is highly likely things would be fairly much as you left them? In other words, how is social order possible? How can societies hang together at least reasonably well, when they are divided along a number of lines, including ethnicity as well as socio-economic lines, which Sociologists commonly refer to as *class*?

Not all Sociologists answer this central question in the same way it should be noted. The French sociologist and philosopher Michel Foucault, for instance, has a different way of pursuing this question from the nineteenth-century 'founders' of the discipline – one that led him to be interested in questions of power and knowledge, especially in the workings of social control institutions such as prisons and hospitals. As he puts it:

Traditional Sociology puts the problem more in these terms: how can a society make individuals live together. I was interested by the opposite problem, or, if you will by the opposite answer to this problem; through what system of exclusion, eliminating whom, creating what division, through what workings of negation and rejection, is society able to function?

(Foucault 1974: 154)

The other side of the equation is the question of how social change occurs. This can be asked at either the macro level of whole societies or the micro level of individual behaviour. Let's consider some examples. At the macro level, recent events in regions as diverse as the Middle East, Asia (especially Afghanistan), and Africa highlight this question. Can major social change occur in these geographical locations without significant bloodshed? What are the possibilities for a relatively peaceful transition from one social order to another? To what extent are those who were in positions of power under old regimes able to relinquish that power under new political circumstances?

Another example is in the COVID-19 pandemic era as we get into a race between the virus and its variants to effectively vaccinate the world's population against its spread. What are the implications of a much greater proportion of people working from home (at least part of the time), for travel and tourism, for the division of labour between partners in a relationship, particularly for women who have incurred the greater burden of economic loss and greater household responsibility? With the newfound respect for teachers generally occasioned by many parents having to undertake home schooling for long periods of time, will that be translated into status and pay improvements for the teaching profession?

Thinking about elements of continuity and change in a society suggests other examples. At the micro level, an example would be the often awkward question of gender relations. Who pays for dinner on a first date? What norms (or behavioural expectations) govern this potentially ambience-shattering issue of who should foot the bill? Traditionally, the man did so without question. Indeed, in more expensive restaurants the menu handed to the woman did not even contain prices. Times have certainly changed. But although the traditional normative expectations of gender relations have changed, nothing definitive has replaced them. Does an invitation to dinner carry an implied offer to meet the cost? What will be expected in return if one person does pay the bill? Is there an implied sexual contract here? What happens if one partner earns more than the other? The matter of payment has to be delicately negotiated on the spot. Perhaps for students, the egalitarianism of poverty resolves the issue in favour of an equal share. But some questions are difficult to ask. In hetero-sexual relationships for instance, it is difficult for a woman to ask, 'Are you the sort of male who still thinks it is appropriate for men to pay for women, so that if I offer to pay half, you will be offended?' 'Should I take from the fact that you held the car door open for me when we went out, that you will also want to pay for dinner?' Students who work as restaurant staff are often instructed to delicately place the bill on the table between the couple and let them sort it out! It's difficult to be 'proper' in this situation where the normative expectations of appropriate gender relations are being renegotiated. Beyond the dynamics of dating for heterosexual couples, we should also ask, how are these questions negotiated for same-sex couples? These are issues of continuity and change, which are of fundamental importance to Sociologists.

Some key questions

For C. Wright Mills (1959: 13), there are three major questions inevitably raised by those with a sociological imagination at the macro, or societal, level of analysis:

- What is the structure of this particular society as a whole and how do the parts relate to one another and to the whole?
- Where does it stand in human history and the development of humanity as a whole?
- What categories of people dominate in society at this par-ticular time and how is that changing?

Think of these questions in relation to recent events in Afghanistan, where a twenty year and 83 billion US dollar attempt to recon-struct the country on behalf of the United States and its allies was all but swept away in a matter of weeks by the Taliban. To under-stand sociologically the tumultuous events which have been unfolding in that geopolitical region now, requires asking these three basic questions above. Wright Mills is quick to point out that other social science disciplines ask these sorts of questions as well, but they are most central to the discipline of Sociology.

What is the structure of Afghani society? Afghanistan is a collection of multi-ethnic and multi-lingual tribal alliances within a series of related geographic regions in the midst of larger powerful states such as Iran, Mongolia, and Pakistan. In recent history Afghani identity has been weakened without a strong central authority such as a stable national government (see Lee 2019) Some Afghanis, through ethnicity, are closer (in terms of national identity) to Iran, some to Mongolia, and others to other parts of central Asia. Following the withdrawal of the Americans and their allies, the national government proved only to be a very weak one. One of the key problems for America and its allies was the assumption that all 'Afghanis' would have loyalty to the idea of Afghanistan that the West tried to create.

Where does Afghanistan stand in human history? Afghanistan is somewhat unique in modernity as a country that has, to a large extent, resisted various forms of sustained colonialism, where many other countries, especially in Asia, have been transformed by Western forces over time through direct impact or through emu-lation. As a country it has never really been conquered by a foreign power such as the French, Russians, British, or Americans, and is unique in many ways in terms of its problems as a nation state.

This leads us to the third of Wright Mills' questions about which people dominate in a society. A key advantage that gave the Taliban such swift momentum in re-establishing itself as rulers in Afghanistan was the corruption of the Afghani national leaders and leaders of regional governments who were quite easily bought off with cash, amnesty, and positions in the Taliban regime itself (*New York Times* 2021) and without feelings of belonging or loyalty to the Afghanistan created by the West. A sociological imagination can give much insight into the out-ward chaos of world events such as those that have occurred in Afghanistan in recent years.

Some Sociologists focus at the closer micro level of analysis, at features within societies. Again, the sociological imagination involves approaching the explanation of social phenomena as sociological problems by asking five basic questions in the quest to understand social phenomena. These questions are:

- What's happening?
- Why?
- What are the consequences?
- How do you know?
- How could it be otherwise?

A couple of examples will make this point clearer. First, let's consider the social and sociological problem of divorce. The death in the United Kingdom of Prince Phillip in 2021 brought to an end his marriage of 72 years to his (distant) cousin Queen Elizabeth: a remarkable achievement (Heald 1991). Yet only a tiny proportion of all marriages last 50 years, let alone 72. In the United States, it's about 7 per cent (Antoniades 2016), with similar minorities in the United Kingdom and in Australia. In Western countries, roughly speaking, for every five marriages registered, between two and three will end in divorce. In Australia, of all relationships that result in marriage, over 40 per cent will end in divorce, although divorce has decreased since 1999 (ABS 2020). Crude divorce rates have, after a pattern of increasing over many years, begun to decline, however.

This is a personal trouble, threatening personal values and creating a great amount of anxiety and stress for all – except perhaps the lawyers involved. But public issues are also at stake. In other words, to seek to understand why this is occurring we must look beyond the level of the individuals involved to ask the broader sociological question: 'What is it about the way our society is organised that results in the situation we have today?' Is staying together more difficult than it once was? Are people more isolated than previously? Does the fact that many couples cohabit before 'tying the knot' increase the likelihood of them staying together? A sociological imagination directs attention away from a focus only on the individuals to the wider context of group behaviour by using the five basic questions above.

To ask, '*What's happening?*' seeks to describe empirically (that is, with evidence drawn from the observable world) what's going on, what patterns exist. With divorce it would mean considering the empirical patterns about divorce from published sources such as those provided by agencies, including national statistical agencies and specialist research institutes on the family such as the Australian Bureau of Statistics and the Australian Institute of Family Studies. Are there peaks in the divorce rate according to the length of marriage? Is the 'seven-year-itch' a real phenomenon? Are couples more likely to divorce if they marry at certain ages?

'*Why do people think and act as they do?*' is the next question to consider. How can these empirical patterns be explained? Why has the rate of marital dissolution reached these levels? But also, why has divorce been declining in recent years? Is it the changing social acceptability of divorce, where in the past, unhappy partners often stayed together 'for the sake of the children'? With the diminishing affordability of entering the housing market in many larger cities there are additional financial pressures, as there are on domestic roles if, for instance, one partner loses their job and has to take up the bulk of the domestic responsibilities? Is it the result of having more families in which both partners have serious careers? Is it greater mobility and more migration, leading couples to live away from other social contacts, such as wider families? Conversely, do all of these factors account for the reduction in divorce rates and couples staying together in recent years?

What are the consequences of this social phenomenon? How does a divorce affect children? Is it better for the parents to stay together 'for the sake of the children' or to separate? How are the arrangements we make in this area changing, such as the more systematic collection of maintenance payments? Is it changing the way we think about long-term marriage to one person throughout our lives? What are the consequences of changing family structure now that the proportion of one-parent families is increasing? In the 34-year period from 1986 to 2020 in

Australia, as a proportion of all families with dependent children, one-parent families have remained between 15 and 19 per cent. In 87 per cent of these, the lone parent was a woman (ABS 2020). A colleague of ours had a child in a primary school class where the children who still live with both their original biological parents were in a distinct minority.

'*How do you know?* ' involves examining the evidence. This requires a scepticism and a reluctance on your part to accept explanations at face value. Does the rising and falling divorce rate indicate an increase and then decrease in the extent of marital unhappiness or, since the passing of no-fault divorce legislation in the 1970s, is divorce a more socially acceptable means of resolving marital unhappiness? Does the divorce rate mean that marriage is 'going out of fashion' and alternatively 'back in fashion'? Given that most divorcees remarry and a large proportion of the population still responds to surveys as 'now married', perhaps it is not marriage itself that is declining but the idea of being married to only one person in your life.

The final question is '*How could it be otherwise?*' What other consequences, patterns and explanations are possible to understand divorce? Given all the pressures there are on people staying together, and the difficulty of expecting one person to meet all one's needs over a lifetime, maybe the question is back to front. Maybe the question to ask is not why 43 per cent of marriages fail, but why the other 57 per cent manage to stay together? As illustrated in the 2007 movie 'License to Wed', should all people intending to commit matrimony be encouraged to undertake some sort of marriage preparation class? Would the personal troubles of divorce be eased if partners were encouraged or even required to enter into a pre-nuptial contract, specifying how marital property would be divided as well as how the custody of children would be organised should the marriage be dissolved? Is formalising the relationship but living in a common law or de facto union, as is increasingly common, more conducive to personal happiness?

The quest for a sociologically adequate explanation of divorce would involve considering all these questions. When thinking about any social issue, these are the sorts of questions to consider in order to begin to analyse that phenomenon sociologically.

Conclusion

This chapter has considered some of the fundamental aspects of sociological explanation and introduced the elements of a sociological imagination as being centrally concerned with the relationship between the individual and society. The distinctive feature of a sociological imagination is a concern to elucidate the relationship between personal troubles at the level of the individual and public issues at the societal level. Sociological, as distinct from social, problems can be found at all levels, from the micro to the macro. At all levels, Sociologists are concerned with explaining the twin problems of continuity and social change. The next chapter will turn to the question of what makes sociological explanation different from other sorts of explanation.

References

ABS (Australian Bureau of Statistics), 2020. 'Marriages and Divorces, Australia'. Australian Bureau of Statistics [www.abs.gov.au/ausstats/abs@.nsf/mf/3310.0].

The Age (newspaper), 2014. 'Boy, 2, accidentally shoots and kills mother in US Walmart', 31 December [www.theage.com.au/world/boy-2-accidentally-shoots-and-kills-mother-in-us-walmart-20141231-12fwzn.html].

Antoniades, C., 2016. 'The secret to a long-lasting marriage' [www.washingtonpost.com/lifestyle/magazine/the-secret-to-a-long-lasting-marriage/2016/02/09/7faefe02-aff8-11e5-9ab0-884d1cc4b33e_story.html].

Baum, F., 1998. 'Private Grief to Public Troubles: Suicide and Public Health'. In Touch: Newsletter of the Public Health, Association of Australia, February, p. 3.

Berger, P., 1963. *An Invitation to Sociology*. Penguin, New York.

Campbell, D., 2020. 'UK Coronavirus Victims Have Lain Undetected at Home for Two Weeks', *Guardian*, 8 June [www.theguardian.com/world/2020/jun/07/uk-coronavirus-victims-have-lain-undetected-at-home-for-two-weeks?CMP=share_btn_link].

Coulson, M., and Riddell, D., 1970. *Approaching Sociology: a Critical Introduction*. Routledge, London.

Elliott, J.R., and Andais, J., 2006. 'Race, Class, and Hurricane Katrina: Social Differences in Human Responses to Disaster', *Social Science Research*, 35:2, 295–321.

Everytown Research, 2020. 'Gun violence and COVID 19 colliding' [https://everytownresearch.org/report/gun-violence-and-covid-19-colliding-public-health-crises/].

Foucault, M., 1974. 'Michel Foucault on Attica' interview, Telos, Spring: 54–61.

Goldthorpe, J., 2016. *Sociology as a Population Science*. Cambridge University Press, Cambridge.

Guardian (newspaper), 2021. 'Man's body found after lying in Norway flat for Nine years', 9 April [www.theguardian.com/world/2021/apr/09/mans-body-was-found-after-lying-in-norway-flat-for-nine-years-say-police].

Heald, T., 1991. *The Duke: a Portrait of Prince Philip*. Hodder and Stoughton, London.

Lee, J.E., 2019. *Afghanistan: a History from 1260 to the Present*. Reaktion Books, London.

New York Times (newspaper), 2021. 'Taliban Sweep in Afghanistan Follows Years of U.S. Miscalculations' *New York Times*, 14 August [www.nytimes.com/2021/08/14/us/politics/afghanistan-biden.html].

O'Day, E., and Heimberg, R., 2021. Social Media Use, Social Anxiety, and Loneliness: a Systematic Review', *Computers in Human Behavior Reports*, 3.

Robertson, I., 1987. *Sociology*, 3rd edn. Worth, New York.

Ronson, J., 2016. *So You've Been Publicly Shamed*. Picador, London

Safe Work Australia, 2019. 'Work-related traumatic injury fatalities Australia 2019' [www.safeworkaustralia.gov.au/doc/work-related-traumatic-injury-fatalities-australia-2019].

Solnick, S., and Hemenway, D., 2019. 'Unintentional Firearm Deaths in the United States 2005–2015', *Injury Epidemiology*, 6:42 [https://doi.org/10.1186/s40621-019-0220-0].

Waters, M., and Crook, R., 1990. *Sociology One*. Longman Cheshire, Melbourne.

Wright Mills, C., 1959. *The Sociological Imagination*. Penguin, New York.

3 Sociology's place in the academy

This chapter considers what makes sociological explanation distinctive from other forms of explanation. These other forms may involve the same focus of study – the relationship between the individual and society – but there is a distinctively sociological way of studying this relationship. In the same way that an object, such as a motor car, may be viewed very differently, depending on whether the viewer is a potential purchaser, a mechanic, a car thief, or an orthopaedic surgeon, there are different approaches to understanding and explaining social life. All scholarship requires selectivity; the focus in this chapter is the distinctively selective approach that is Sociology.

The science of Sociology

The task of differentiating sociological explanation from other explanations or types of knowledge usually involves some claim about the scientific status of sociological knowledge; in other words, that Sociology is a science – a social science. What does it mean to say that Sociology is a social science? In what ways can it be considered scientific? Such questions have been the subject of considerable debate within the discipline and they relate to the philosophical underpinnings of Sociology.

The philosophy of science, and the social sciences in particular, is well explored in other texts (for an introduction to the issues, see Rosenberg 2016). For our purposes, we will briefly outline two major positions. These are known usually as either hard or

DOI: 10.4324/9781003316329-3

soft science approaches, or by their roughly equivalent philo-sophical names of *positivist* and *non-positivist* (sometimes called *naturalistic*) approaches. Most Sociologists work within one of these two approaches.

The first view, the positivist approach to this question of how the sociological study of society is scientific, is to argue that science is something done by other disciplines such as chem-istry and biology. To study society scientifically, Sociology can and should emulate these other disciplines as far as possible. This view is succinctly expressed by the English sociologist John Goldthorpe (1974: 3):

> Sociology is the study of human social behaviour. It represents an attempt to apply to the study of human society, the same scientific method and approach that has been so dramatically successful in yielding an understanding of the physical world.

Working within this approach to the discipline, Sociologists have attempted to develop the same sort of law-like statements found in the natural and physical sciences. Some of these are well established. An example would be that the internal solidarity of a group varies with the degree of the external threat. One often hears older members of a community remark, 'We were never so unified as a nation as during the two world wars' – a time when the external threat to our society was at its greatest. This is an expression of the law-like statement above. Furthermore, identi-fying a common enemy can be a political strategy for attempting to improve internal solidarity with a view to being re-elected, as appears to be happening in many Western countries in relation to the supposed 'threat' of China.

Historically speaking, changes in internal solidarity have been reflected in parallel changes in other aspects of society, such as suicide rates. A contemporary expression of this insight, deriving from one of the 'founding fathers' of positivist Sociology, Emile Durkheim (1970) is the apparently counter-intuitive finding that rates of suicide in the COVID-19 pandemic have not actually increased (at least so far) (see the *New Daily* 2021). Durkheim argued that suicide was related to the degree of social integration that individuals felt with the society around them. Events such as wars, depressions, and indeed pandemics may lead to people feeling more integrated, not less, and a part of the effort to overcome the threat to the wellbeing of society as a whole. So in times of war, the suicide rate has gone down (O'Malley 1975). Some governments today have tried to invoke the war metaphor against the pandemic ('we're at war with the virus here'), while others (such as New Zealand) have invoked a team metaphor ('the team of five million', see Cave 2020). Durkheim referred to the degree of social solidarity as being important and these invocations can be seen as attempts to increase the level of social solidarity. Another example comes from Northern Ireland. Since the signing of the Peace Accord in 1998, and its electoral ratification, there has been a marked reduction in paramilitary violence. Since then, also, the number of young people turning the violence on themselves by committing suicide has dramatically increased. Commentators have indicated that 'the troubles' had a protective role, especially for young men, in providing a sense of solidarity. With that role diminished, and with unemployment high, a sense of purposelessness has resulted (*New Statesman* 2020).

Further application of this law-like statement can be made with reference to whole societies. Take, for example, the European Union. Europe, from the early modern period up to the Second World War, had been a continent riven by constant economic, social, and political conflict as social change and emerging national interests collided, resulting in continual threat to the continent's stability. The catastrophies of the two world wars that impacted terribly on the whole continent was for many law makers, leaders, and citizens a catalyst to try and engender political and economic unity to offset further threats of an individual nation dominating the continent. Russian aggression in Eastern Europe, especially the invasion of Ukraine, is a recent example and one that is leading to much greater unity amongst EU nations faced with the external threat of Russia. Another argument for European unity and internal solidarity is to combat economic changes such as the globalisation of production where smaller European nations under the protection of the EU have some recourse to economic assistance during downturns. This has been the experience of countries such as Greece. The complex legal, economic, and political agreements that define the European Union have come under increasing scrutiny of late, with individual nations such as the United Kingdom withdrawing from the EU, due at least in some part to feelings that they are economically and politically better off being independent.

Or perhaps in the context of climate change leading to global warming, the generalised threat to the future of humankind may eventually lead to more internal solidarity between nations to combat such changes to the physical and human ecosystems? However, the evidence from attempts thus far, such as the various international summits and protocols, to find common ground and a basis for collective action to both mitigate and adapt to rising global temperatures, does not give grounds for confidence that this will occur; at least not until the threat is much more obvious and being more widely felt.

The more threatened a group is (be it a small-scale group such as a family or a larger group such as a whole nation), the more likely it will tend to concentrate on those things that bind its members together rather than divide them. For example, in the post-Cold War era (roughly 1946–91), when the threat of nuclear holocaust eased, there was a period when the perceived external threat to whole societies, such as Australia or the United States, lessened. As a result, some major internal divisions surfaced with renewed vigour and have continued apace with rapid economic and technological changes characterising a transformed economic and political landscape. It is possible to say that the major threat to the security of these countries is as much internal as it is external. Intensifying social divisions along racial and income lines (as the polarisation into rich and poor rapidly continues) threaten national stability. Very recently in the United States, this has occurred to the point where the violence taking place, particularly in the large cities and especially amongst young men, is something akin to a civil war in which the victims might be considered urban war wounded. In other words, as the external threat receded, internal solidarity decreased.

The trend has affected other areas of society, including politics. Political cultures tend to work on the basis of the construction of what we call an *outgroup* – a 'they' or an 'other'. In the United States, for example, since the end of the Cold War the 'other' has changed. The threat previously came from outside American society (for example, the Russians). Then the 'other' of American politics became more focused internally, on groups such as immigrants or ultra-conservative political groups as seen by the bombing of a government building in Oklahoma in 1995, resulting in a huge loss of life. It changed again with the events of 11 September 2001 and the emergence of terrorist groups such as Al Qaeda – a development that led to the establishment of a government bureaucracy for 'homeland security'. A similar trend has been apparent in countries such as the United Kingdom, Canada, France, Germany, and Australia, first with the emergence of ultra conservative political parties constructing the 'other' on the basis of ethnicity – First Nations peoples and immigrants, especially those arriving illegally by boat from countries like Syria, Iraq, Afghanistan, and Sri Lanka. More recently, especially since events such as the various incidents of Islamist violence like the Charlie Hebdo shootings, attention has focused on internal security issues. Internal threats are also exemplified by acts of domestic terrorism such as the Christchurch Mosque shootings and the storming of the United States Congress after the 2020 presidential election. It can be seen by these examples that internal solidarity and external threat are closely related. And this is the 'hard science' answer to the question of the scientific nature of Sociology, modelling the discipline on other sciences in the search for law-like statements.

The alternative is the non-positivist approach, sometimes called the naturalistic or soft science approach. From this position the objects of study in the biological and physical sciences are so different from those in the social sciences that different methods of inquiry or research techniques are necessary. The quest for sociological understanding is still scientific in character but what makes it scientific is not so much the particular methods used but the approach taken. This view has been discussed by Berger (1963) as the humanist approach to the philosophical questions about how we can 'know' things, in this case, about the social world. It is the manner of proceeding in a disciplined fashion that gives Sociology, and indeed other social sciences, a scientific character. It is a way of proceeding that seeks explanations for social phenomena based on a rational appeal to impartial evidence. After all, this is what is meant when we describe Sociology as a *scholarly discipline* in either a positivist or non-positivist mode: studying social phenomena in a particular way that is systematic, rigorous and based on the use of evidence about the world. The question of what constitutes evidence will be taken up in a later chapter. An example should make clearer the difference between the biological and physical sciences on one hand and the social sciences on the other. In the former, propositions about the physical world are expressed as laws – mechanical and invariant. Whether it occurs in Melbourne or Chicago, in 1921 or 2021, if you sit directly under a very ripe apple hanging on a tree, sooner or later you will get a lump on the head. This will occur irrespective of whether a chap called Newton ever lived or ever developed a theory of gravity to explain why this lump will occur.

Law-like statements, however, such as the example given above, while useful, are limited in social life. Sociologists working within a positivist approach, attempting to emulate their natural and physical scientist colleagues, have found a relatively narrow range of areas where such statements are applicable. For the most part, they have to contend with the fact that people do things differently in different parts of the world; that actions and behaviours have different meanings within different cultures. A couple of examples may make this point clearer. One example concerns the meaning of 'dinner'. In North America 'dinner' is for refuelling the body and is usually served soon after six o'clock in the evening. It is typically one course, with all the food on one plate, served without alcohol, and completed inside half an hour. There are, of course, exceptions, but this is how most people there take their main meal of the day. In Europe, by contrast, the meaning of dinner is cast not only around refuelling but also as a means of socialising. Eaten later (as late as nine or ten o'clock in countries such as Spain), it involves several courses over more than an hour, with alcohol consumed by everyone, even by children, who drink it in small quantities or diluted. In North America giving your child a glass of wine with dinner would be defined by many as akin to child abuse! Australasia, at the crossroads of these two cultures, has adopted some dining customs from each. In some Australian households dinner may be eaten at different times, depending on other commitments. For some it may be eaten in front of the television while for others an emphasis is put on the family sitting down together around a dining table and eating while catching up with the day's events. In other words, in attempting to understand behaviour we cannot take for granted that the meaning of actions is always the same.

Another example is the social construction of the meaning of the categories of plants and animals that are known as 'weeds' and 'vermin'. Under what circumstances does a plant or animal come to be defined as such, and how does that definition change over time? The pejorative meaning (inviting justified destruction) varies over time, between societies and within different geographical areas. Pests and weeds from this point of view can be defined as animals and plants that just happen to be in the wrong place. Think of the 'positioning' of plants and animals, be they dingoes, cane toads, gorse or *pinus radiata* trees. Or the difference in the positioning of possums in Australia and New Zealand – cute furry little native animals in the former; bloody pests wreaking untold ecological damage and a resource to be made into garments in the other. One country's pest may be another's endangered species! Likewise, it is challenging to one's sense of being an Australian when you visit places, such as California, where you are harangued by the locals about those iconic trees of the Australian bush, the *Eucalyptus* species, being weeds. Even the social meaning attributed to an object or item can vary according to the circumstance. Consider the plant *Papaver rhoeas*, an annual herbaceous species of the poppy family known variously as the corn poppy, red poppy, Flanders poppy or Remembrance poppy. It grows in many countries, in disturbed soil, and is known as a weed for its invasion of crops such as corn. Since the First World War more than a century ago, it has taken on a particular significance after it was observed growing around graves and trenches. Especially in Commonwealth countries it has come to be regarded as a sacred symbol of sacrifice, and a

cloth or paper version worn as a lapel in clothing to commem-
orate wartime events.

   To return to the gravity example, in the physical sciences it
is absurd to ask what the apple *means* by falling. In the social
sciences, by contrast, to ask what the meaning is of different
actions, such as smiling, is a very important question. Also, apples
continue to fall independent of our knowledge of the theory of
gravity, whereas people may and often do change their behaviour as a result of sociological knowledge. Think of the roles of
men and women in Western society. In very recent history there
has been a gradual recognition by many women, and some men,
that beliefs about what is 'natural' for men and women to do
beyond the basic facts of human reproduction are not in some
way biologically determined as was once believed, but are socially
constructed. That is, they derive culturally from our understanding
of how the world works. Think, for example, how far we have
come since the nineteenth century when the prevailing belief,
strongly reinforced by the doctors of the time, was an insistence
that a woman's ovaries determined her physical, intellectual, and
emotional behaviour. This belief was used by men to oppose
women studying at university and to exclude them from entering
professions such as medicine (Smith-Rosenberg and Rosenberg
1973). When these theories were proved to be nonsense, ovaries
went on working as they had always done, but women began to
behave differently, demanding the right to vote, to receive a university education, and to work in a wider range of occupations,
including the professions. A social movement towards changing
relations between the sexes was thus set in motion and has been
one of the really important areas of social change in the past
century. In other words, there are crucial differences in the subject matters of the physical and biological sciences on one hand
and the social sciences on the other. Because of these differences,
different methods of going about studying each are necessary. To
put it another way, there cannot be a unity of scientific method
between the physical and social sciences. The subject matter is
sufficiently different to require different methods of investigation. What then makes the sociological quest a scientific one in
either its 'hard science' or 'soft science' mode? As Peter Berger

(1963: 27) argues, it is the particular way the understanding of society is approached:

> The sociologist then is someone concerned with understanding society in a disciplined way. The nature of the discipline is scientific ... one of the main characteristics of this scientific frame of reference is that operations are bound by certain rules of evidence.

The concern is with *empirical* evidence – evidence based on observable experience of the social world, in order to back up claims made about the social world. We explore this idea of evidence in greater depth with reference to how we collect and use evidence in Chapter 8.

Distinguishing sociological explanation

At this stage in the quest, to understand the nature of sociological explanation, we can begin by distinguishing it from types of knowledge that are *metaphysical*, that is, not empirically based. Sociological explanation can be distinguished from all non-empirically based types of knowledge, such as fortune-telling, and also from religious knowledge. For example, the existence of a supernatural being such as God in the Christian religion, as usually conceived, cannot be empirically established. One either takes it on the basis of faith or not. Nothing in Sociology is taken on faith (which is not to say that many Sociologists in their personal lives are not themselves religious). This follows from the emergence of the discipline as a distinctively modern, secular knowledge of human society and human social relationships during the period following the two revolutions we spoke about in the introduction. This emergence was only possible in a world that had rejected the absolute basis of any religious authority.

How can Sociology be distinguished from other pursuits such as journalism? Both activities analyse what is occurring in society, and some journalists display effective sociological imagination. But in general they analyse society in different ways. First, Sociology claims a kind of knowledge about society that is *objective*, in the sense of being impartial and independent. In contrast, journalists, broadly speaking, write about society in a way determined by the need to sell newspapers or maintain ratings. At times, therefore, they may be less than objective in terms of the stories chosen for investigation and reporting, or the need to avoid casting the owners of the media outlet in an unfavourable light. Second, by writing about the world around us and about what we call commonsense knowledge and understanding of that world, the approach to writing is somewhat different. Journalists, for the most part, use commonsense concepts to analyse this social world, which itself is riddled with prejudices, especially cultural ones. Sociologists, on the other hand, attempt to escape (with varying degrees of success) these limitations with demands for logical argument, empirical evidence and, most importantly, the use of a precise language to analyse what is occurring.

The frequent use by Sociologists of a somewhat different language from the one journalists use to analyse social life raises the so-called jargon issue. Already in this book a considerable number of terms have been highlighted that may not be familiar to a newcomer to the discipline. While all occupational groups use a specialised language, Sociology is sometimes criticised for using an obscure language to talk about things that are assumed to be commonsense. While the use of a specialised language can and sometimes is overdone or carried to unnecessary lengths, its use is important as it is aiming at a more exact, precise, and thus more satisfactory, understanding of the phenomenon in question. Much sociological insight is what Randall Collins (1982: vi) calls 'non-obvious'. He argues:

> Sociology does know some important principles of how the world operates. These are not just matters of conceptualisation and definition. They tell us why things happen in certain ways rather than others, and they go beyond the surface of ordinary belief. The principles had to be discovered by professional scholars, including some of the major thinkers of the past; they are by no means obvious.

Sociological concepts and a more specialised language generally are some of the tools by which these sociological insights are achieved and which differentiate Sociology from journalism. Their use facilitates the process of *generalisation*, crucial to the search for patterns and ultimately to the sociological quest. Asking the question, 'To what extent can we generalise?' involves addressing the question of how much of what occurs to individuals can be said to apply also to groups. Sociologists are cautious about overgeneralising and the use of a more specialised and precise language is a means by which they pursue this caution. Consider some examples beginning with the terminology frequently used to describe groups in our society. These terms may include 'bougie' (or 'boujee), 'geek', 'queer', 'bogan', 'homie', 'noob', 'millennial' or 'gen z' to name just a few. These terms are not usually carefully deployed and are often used to label whole groups of people who have little in common, or are used in a way that says as much about those applying the label as those to whom the label is supposed to apply. Crucial to the quest for sociological understanding of the individual and society is this concern with careful enunciation of exactly what one is talking about. A specialised language is the result. A social media example of how this can go awry stands as a cautionary tale of effective communication based on knowledge and application of some terms. Some older users of social media have misinterpreted certain short hand used on social media such as 'LOL' (laugh out loud) to stand for 'lots of love'. When friends or family have posted unfortunate or unhappy news, some older users wishing to show empathy and support have posted 'LOL' in response, unaware of the conventional meaning of the acronym. Long correspondences attempting to clear up the misunderstanding ensue!

An example of the need for a specialised language is the ambiguity with which the term 'ethnic' is often used in everyday language to apply to all people whose family background in the society to which they have migrated is less than two generations and whose original language was not English. The use of this term, however, is based on a misunderstanding of ethnicity. Everyone has an ethnic background – long-term residents as much as more recent arrivals. Aiming at precision, Sociologists commonly refer to the above group as people of non-English speaking background (often using the acronym NESB). We also need to be aware of how the term is caught up in what are basically political and social processes of inclusion or exclusion from social groups.

The need for precision as a basis for analysis is also evident when new aspects of the social organisation of a society become apparent, for which we may lack a suitable term or concept. Some examples will illustrate this point. Of all those couples who married in 2017 in Australia, 81 per cent had cohabited prior to marriage. This compares to 16 per cent of couples who got married in 1975 (AIFS 2021). How would you introduce a person with whom you are emotionally involved in a cohabiting, de facto relationship but with whom you have not actually committed matrimony? People in this category are a sizeable group of the population. 'This is my boyfriend/girlfriend' is hardly appropriate when you are in your twenties (or forties). 'My lover/mistress' may be a bit old-fashioned. 'My room mate' hardly conveys the exact nature of your relationship. 'My spouse' has overtones of wedding bells. 'My bedmate' may not be exactly what you want. 'My beau' or 'my significant other' are occasionally used. Perhaps 'my partner' is beginning to fill the gap in the language. But until a term comes to have a commonsense meaning which everyone understands, the awkwardness of the need to state the extent of your pairing with someone continues.

A second example of a need for appropriate terms that has been slow to emerge is with gender. Rising awareness of diverse gendered identities of individuals is commensurate with the development of more accurate and inclusive terminology. Typically this is emerging with the display of personal pronouns such as she/her, he/him, and they/their. Or indeed without a definite label denoting a more genderqueer or fluid identity. In some instances, such as with those with Latin American heritage in the United States, gender and ethnicity have intersected in language moving beyond strictly gendered terms such as Latina and Latino to Latinx for example.

Not only do we lack appropriate terms in some areas, but those that are used in everyday life may be subject to ambiguous usage. An example is the term 'profession'. It is widely used in its commonsense meaning to refer to supposedly special sorts of occupations more worthy and of higher status than mere jobs.

The usage is very confused, however. Indeed, it is frequently claimed by occupations in an attempt to secure certain advantages in the labour market: 'We are a profession and therefore ...' is a common expression of this view. Using the term in relation to occupations traditionally thought of as professions, such as medicine and law is not controversial, but beyond that the agreement ends. Not only do we have the 'world's oldest profession' (sex workers) laying claim to the title but in recent years a range of occupations as diverse as jockeys and salespersons have laid claim to the term. Aiming at precision, Sociologists have tried to refine the usage of the term, though there is considerable disagreement about what the defining characteristics should be. The most common view perhaps, espoused by the American sociologist Eliot Freidson (1986: 123), is that the term should refer only to those whose livelihood is earned on the basis of credentials (qualifications, etc.) that they have gained through higher education. The original meaning is used but it is now carefully defined.

Then there are terms which become out of date but are still used for a lack of a suitable alternative. Describing countries as belonging to 'the third world' is one such term, which is no longer appropriate these days. Formerly the term referred to those poorer countries, usually less 'developed', in Asia, Africa, and Central and South America, whose economies were still heavily dependent on agriculture. But it no longer makes sense to refer to the first or second worlds (despite the popular refrain of 'first world problem!'). Nor is 'developed' or 'underdeveloped' a particularly useful distinction – many countries of the former Soviet empire under any criteria would be considered in the category of what used to be called 'third world' on the basis of development. Likewise, some countries that formerly were in the underdeveloped group, such as Singapore, now have per capita incomes that exceed those in some formerly 'first world' countries such as New Zealand. Clearly some term that precisely describes the relationship between different countries in a manner which reflects wide spread recent social and economic change is needed. Terminology that has emerged more recently is to make a distinction between 'the Global North' and the 'Global South'. So, in common with other academic disciplines, Sociology has developed a specialised language to help in accurately analysing social life. As a result, journalistic and sociological accounts of the same phenomenon can read quite differently, in part because of the different purposes for which they are written.

Sociological explanation must also be differentiated from the sorts of explanations provided by other academic disciplines. The study of society is not the exclusive preserve of Sociology but is a feature of all social sciences. How does sociological explanation differ from those of related social sciences? The areas of overlap are considerable: the study of social life cannot be easily compartmentalised so the boundaries between disciplines are loosely drawn. The difference is more often a matter of emphasis and orientation resulting from their different historical origins than of substance. To return to the spectacles metaphor from earlier, they are different ways of seeing. Wearing a particular set of spectacles brings certain aspects into focus, while fading others more in the background.

Psychology is perhaps the academic discipline with which Sociology is most often confused, though many psychologists prefer to designate themselves as behavioural, rather than social, scientists. Certainly when asked what Sociology is, people often contrast it with Psychology to differentiate its approach. The discipline of Psychology in some ways bridges the natural and social sciences; its specialties range from Neuropsychology at the end of the spectrum closest to Biology, to Behavioural and Social Psychology at the end closest to Sociology. In so far as it is possible to generalise about such a diverse discipline, Psychology is more concerned with the study of individual human social behaviour, while Sociology delves more into group or collective social behaviour, as well as how the individual relates to the whole. One way to distinguish between sociological and other types of explanation is to return to the example of suicide. Emile Durkheim (the first to have the occupational title 'Sociologist'), in his famous work *Suicide* (1970 [1897]), took what many consider to be the supremely individual act of taking one's own life and explained its occurrence with reference to one's belonging to or estrangement from social groups. Psychological explanations focus on individual factors like the state of mind of the person concerned. Durkheim, by the use of data about suicide, was able to show that (in addition to these individual factors) there are distinctly social patterns that are associated with who commits suicide; the age and gender of the person, their religion, and their socio-economic status, among a range of factors. This seminal, groundbreaking research largely holds up today. So the focus is upon the fact of people's membership of social groups. The patterns in Durkheim's work did not relate to the individual frame of mind of those who do commit suicide. This is not to say these questions are not relevant or important; just that the sociological focus is different. As with the boundaries between all social science disciplines, there is a considerable area of overlap between Sociology and Psychology. Small-group Sociology shades into Social Psychology, with its focus on how the social context of behaviour shapes personality and individual behaviour. It is common in universities for Social Psychology to be taught within Sociology departments. Sociology and Psychology also share some of their historic influences. Sigmund Freud, better known as a founding parent of modern Psychology, is also important to the discipline of Sociology.

One area of difference between the two disciplines is in the traditional focus taken in the major intellectual debate about the relative importance of hereditary factors and the environment in determining behavioural outcomes. Is the way a child turns out when they grow up more the result of nature or nurture? Is the outcome because of what they inherit or what Sociologists call the process of *socialisation*? It is a complex debate and difficult to summarise accurately in a brief treatise. While both disciplines acknowledge the importance of both sides of the debate, it is generally the case that psychologists (at least those who study behaviour) tend to stress the interaction between the biological aspects (especially response and instinct) and the social (their term being 'social conditioning') aspects. By contrast, Sociologists tend to stress the social environment. Sociologists tend to emphasise how individual uniqueness is shaped by social life, particularly relationships with others, and especially those relationships beyond direct face-to-face ones. Sociologists tend to argue that we do not get very far in our understanding of human behaviour by

considering only the properties of individuals; rather, it is necessary to consider the interaction of the individual with the society
of which that individual is a part, especially the relationships that
directly connect people. The implications of failing to do this will
be addressed later in this chapter.

How does Sociology differ from the other social sciences?
Political science takes as its main emphasis the political aspects of
the organisation of society, focusing especially on the manner in
which power is manifested in the organisation of society through
political behaviour and different forms of government. *Geography*
draws on Sociology and other social sciences in order to inform
its orientation towards the study of relationships between the
physical and human world. *Economics* concentrates on the economic relationships that exist between individuals and between
groups of individuals of all sizes, from small numbers of people
to whole nations. The study of how goods and services are
produced, distributed, and consumed involves examining the
economic aspects of social life.

The closest relatives to Sociology are history and anthropology. *History* is particularly close to Sociology as both these
social sciences, in general, have become more concerned with
understanding the historical antecedents of social organisation of
various kinds. This issue of identifying the historical antecedents
is one of the ways in which sociologist C. Wright Mills has identified the centrality of the study of the relationship between the
individual and society as the hallmark of the sociological imagination. For him, this involves the study of the relationship between
biography and history: the place of individual biographies in
the larger scheme of things, which necessarily has an historical
component.

With *anthropology*, Sociology has perhaps the closest relationship, often being institutionally located within the same university
department. From its origins in the study of other cultures in the
era of colonialism (it used to be said that anthropologists studied
only those societies that didn't have dry-cleaning), anthropology
has now effectively become comparative Sociology. Taking culture as one of its central organising foci and, nowadays, studying
both non-industrial, First Nations, and non-Western societies as

well as their own society, many social anthropologists are indistinguishable from their sociologist colleagues.

In some universities Sociology is located with *social work*,
but the two are not the same even though they are sometimes
assumed to be so. As Peter Berger (1963: 15) has argued, social
work is a practice in society whereas Sociology is more of an
attempt to understand society. Sociology is one of the disciplines (along with Psychology) in which aspiring social workers
should receive training. But there is nothing inherent in the aim
of understanding how the social world works that inevitably leads
to a particular practice. This fact notwithstanding, as we explain
in depth in Chapter 9, sociological knowledge and skills can be
applied to great effect to a range of industries and professions.

So, sociological explanation can be distinguished from other
forms of explanation, both of a social scientific nature and of
an unscientific nature. From the latter, differentiation is possible
because sociological explanation depends on the use of empirical evidence. For other social sciences, while acknowledging the
considerable overlap between the different disciplines, and, in
some senses, the artificial nature of the distinctions anyway, the
difference between sociological and other types of explanation is
largely one of emphasis.

Social structure

Like all the social sciences, Sociology is concerned with the relationship between the individual and society. The uniqueness of
the sociological, though, compared with other sorts of explanation, lies in the manner in which the understanding of social
phenomena is sought in the organisation of society as a whole –
usually referred to as the *social structure* of society. This concept is
defined in terms of the patterns of relationships, which are both
persistent and systematic, between the different parts of a society.

The social structure is comprised of different *social institutions*
that are regular, organised patterns of social behaviour, such as
universities or hospitals. Social structure and social institutions,
it is important to note, are not fixed, unchanging, monolithic
entities resulting in a neat organisation of society. Rather, they

allow for fluidity, diversity, and conflict, as well as change in the sense of taking on new forms. Furthermore, focusing on the social structural level of analysis is not to deny the relevance of an understanding of the activities of individuals, but to argue for the primacy (what comes first) of the group level of analysis. Hence the concept of the social structure is a crucial one for Sociology, acting as a kind of signpost to the kinds of questions to be asked, in particular, 'What is it about the way our society is organised that results in this or that phenomenon occurring?'

Contradiction

The social structural feature of sociological explanation raises the issue of the extent to which the relationship between the individual and society may be a conflictual one. The notion of *contradiction* (sometimes called a *tension* or *paradox*) is an important one in the social sciences. The foundations of this issue are philosophical, based on this important question: What extent of group-level organisation is most consistent with individual freedom and happiness? Or put another way: What sort of controls on individuals are necessary in order to maximise the so-called 'common good'? This vexed and complex question has to do with the relationship of the individual to the larger society.

Consider again as we did in the previous chapter, the recent society-individual tensions around mask wearing when in public places as a public health strategy to reduce the spread of COVID-19. In some countries, wearing a mask had been mandated and in others only highly recommended, yet in almost all countries certain individuals have refused to wear them against sound public health advice. A similar problem exists around vaccinations against COVID-19, and for children against certain other diseases.

Similarly, conflicts within body corporate committees that manage apartment living or between neighbours, generally over privacy issues, are now an everyday occurrence in high density inner urban environments. To what extent should people be allowed to play loud music late at night, burn garbage in their backyards, keep several large guard dogs who bark at the constant sounds of other people, build extensions onto their houses which block out the sun for neighbours, or put up so many Christmas lights that the neighbours complain?

The need to surrender some individuality in the interests of social harmony is well recognised. Should one light a fire on a cold evening when a smog alert for the city has been broadcast? Already in some cities the aesthetic pleasure of an open fire is banned on the grounds of pollution. As inner-city populations increase it is inevitable that someone will end up with their windows only a few metres from someone else's chimney, so the former may get a house full of smoke every time their neighbours light a fire. Similarly, in many places the police will act on complaints about loud parties and eventually confiscate your sound equipment if you don't turn down the sound. In some cities there exist what we call institutional mechanisms (that is, an organisation specially designed for this purpose), which are in effect neighbourhood conflict-resolution centres – neighbours in dispute meet with a trained negotiator, who attempts to resolve the conflict. It seems inevitable that as population densities continue to increase, regulation over disturbing the privacy of others will also continue to rise.

Another example is the festival of Halloween. Processes of globalisation have meant that the festival is 'catching on' in Australasia, but there is a long way to go before it is celebrated with what can only be described as the fervour of North Americans. A contradiction has developed between the traditional and the modern with the rituals involved in the observance of this children's festival. The rituals require children to engage in behaviours which normally they are taught not to do. 'Trick or treating' involves going out in the dark, accepting gifts from strangers and, generally, in the name of 'fun', celebrating aspects of the supernatural that are in some respects at least inimical to established religions.

Or take tourism. As a source of revenue, tourism has become increasingly important for many countries starved of hard currency or undergoing transformation of their traditional income sources. Revenue from tourism throughout the world is now many billions of dollars each year, yet tourist preferences are fickle – a fashionable destination one year may not be popular the next. The Indonesian island of Bali since the October 2002 bombing is a good example of a once-popular tourist destination that suffered from an unforeseen downturn, as are many Asian countries in the wake of events such as various terrorist bombings in Indonesia, the SARS epidemic of 2003, and ongoing political unrest in Thailand and, in very recent times, the global COVID-19 pandemic. The tourist *gaze* (or way of looking) involves a search for authenticity, which is why 'undiscovered' locations are favoured (see Urry 1990). As these places become fashionable, the paradox is that the authenticity is likely to be compromised by the increased numbers of visitors wanting to share the 'authentic' experience, especially as the local people become organised to take advantage of the income possibilities that tourism brings. Trekking in Nepal is an example that comes to mind. Likewise, 'ecotourism' – the search for pristine natural environments, which is likely to place at risk the very rationale for people going there in the first place. Examples of this are the Great Barrier Reef in Australia and Mt Everest in the Himalayan region of Nepal. The Italian city of Venice is an example of the built environment sagging (quite literally) under the weight of mass tourism and compromising the city's delicate infrastructure and historic buildings, while earning an estimated 3 billion Euros for the city a year (*New York Times* 2020). Striking a balance between preservation of the environment and conservation of the species within it, and exploiting it for tourism as well as general development purposes, is a difficult task.

An associated issue is the example of the consequences caused by world population growth, now at the point where food security issues and the ongoing potential for undernourishment (if not starvation) is the lot of probably the majority of the world's people. This situation occurs at a time when agricultural 'overproduction' in the advanced economies is a major source of concern, with primary producers struggling to survive in the face of these huge food surpluses. As well, overnourishment and its consequences are major health problems facing wealthy countries, with a huge industry having grown up around assisting people in those countries to lose weight. To make sense of such a situation it is essential to have an understanding of issues of social structure which includes the power relations between countries of the world. Food is a commodity to be bought and sold. Apart from some gifts of food in the form of aid, the ability of a low-income country to feed its people depends on its ability to pay for the commodities needed, or at least be given credit to do so.

Speaking of the paradoxes of food, a final example. On a visit to the 'Emerald Isle', a visitor learning about the terrible set of events that is usually known as the great Irish Famine of 1845–52 when potato crops failed, cannot help but be struck by a shocking, and indeed in many respects appalling, paradox. In the midst of the starvation that depopulated the Irish countryside as well as spurred outmigration to other countries such as the United States, some of the produce of Irish land that would have saved many of the local inhabitants from starvation was being exported to Britain by Anglo-Irish landowners. Such a paradox or contradiction can only be explained by referring to the Irish social structure of the time, especially the relative position in the social hierarchy (what Sociologists usually call the class structure) of the Anglo-Irish landowners and the poverty stricken landless Irish populace(see O'Neill 2009). So the landowners grew rich while the poor starved.

So the notion of contradiction or paradox is an important one to the social sciences in general and Sociology in particular. The paradoxes and contradictions involved in urban living, Halloween, ecotourism, overpopulation, and food supply illustrate the complex ways in which the individual and society are related.

Society and the individual

The concern to link individual behaviour to its broader social context is the distinguishing feature of the sociological quest and an essential one in understanding the complexities of the social world in which we live. In particular, it enables us to understand and counter the trend towards individualism, which has become a prevalent feature of contemporary life in the advanced economies and complex social structures of the West. This view has grown from a type of 'pop Psychology' that has fuelled a preoccupation, even obsessive belief, in the ability of the study of the life of individuals to provide a sufficient framework for understanding the complexities of human social life. Look in any bookshop or on website at the number of books and posts available promising self-awareness and self-help. Solutions to complex social problems are held to be found in individual actions, which may derive from particular individual failings. Political life is held to be simply explainable only, or mainly, in terms of the behaviours and personalities of individual politicians. Human conflict is frequently held to be the result of poor socialisation or the impulses of individuals. (For a broader account of this phenomenon see Beck and Beck-Gernsheim 2002.)

The consequences of rampant individualism are felt in a number of spheres in society. One is the vulgarisation of the concept of 'rights'. Any problem, any grievance, any failure to get satisfaction can be cast in the discourse of rights and become the subject of litigation. Such an emphasis on solving the tension between the individual and society in favour of the individual is antisocial, in the classic sense of tipping the balance too far in favour of the individual. Concern with individual rights is important but the tension between the individual and the collective cannot be resolved by a narcissistic overemphasis on the individual alone. Arguably, commitments to some notion of 'civic duty', to mutual respect and to responsibility to society are important if our lives are not to be made into survival courses and our cities into combat zones in a dog-eat-dog world. A prime example of this situation was the strong resistance to vaccination and mask wearing to reduce the COVID-19 infection rate.

The nineteenth-century sociologist Emile Durkheim coined the term 'conscience collective' (i.e. collective consciousness) to refer to those aspects of living in group life that require surrendering aspects of individuality in the interests of social harmony and cohesion. Arguably this has declined as individualism has increased, so social order is undermined. Take, for example, how what is defined as 'acceptable' behaviour has changed in what is called the *normative expectations* of watching a movie at your local cinema complex. On recent visits all of the following were observed: loud mobile phone conversations, running discussions on the plot, a domestic dispute voiced in loud, heated whispers, the smell of takeaway food such as curries or pizzas, which permeated the entire theatre, and patrons going in and out of the theatre several times during the screening. One polite request for others to remain quiet was met with the rejoinder that if that particular person wanted to watch it in silence why didn't they watch it at home on a streaming service! It seems that public theatres have become an extension of people's living rooms and domestic life is carried on as it is in private.

In the economic sphere, free-market economic rationalists argue that the best interests of society as a whole will be served by the individual and the unrestrained pursuit of self-interest with an absolute minimum of governmental intervention. In the case of free-market economic policies, as a seminal United Nations report concluded, while it is clear these policies are capable of economic growth, 'it is far from clear they are capable of creating just, civilised and sustainable human societies'. This is the result of 'insufficient account being taken of the effects [of these policies] on the poor, the vulnerable and on the environment' (UNICEF 1994: ch. 3). Recent experiences of what has come to be known as the Global Financial Crisis (GFC) and the economic chaos as a result of the pandemic would bear this out.

Individualism is a powerful example in modern life of what we call an *ideology*. An ideology can be defined as a set of ideas that justifies a course of action; that is, it acts to rationalise a course of action in the sense of underpinning a preferred explanation or understanding with the sense of right and propriety. The emphasis on individualism isolates the individual from their social context. This recalls the famous utterance by the former British prime minister, Margaret Thatcher, when challenged on the effects her government's policies were having on the social fabric of British society as a whole: 'There is no such thing as society' (Thatcher 2013). Denying the relevance (or even existence) of community or society, ignores, or at least gives inadequate attention to, the collective level of analysis, as if an individual can somehow exist apart from this wider societal context.

The whole is more than the sum of its parts. A football team can be no more thought of as just a group of individuals than a whole nation can be understood by the sum of the individuals that comprise it. This is to recall the catch cry of the coaches of sporting teams across the globe, who in their half time 'pep-talks' remind players that 'there is no 'I' in the word team'. The relationships between the individuals in either a football team or a nation are of great importance in adequately accounting for what is going on. In the case of the football team, also important are the club's traditions, the levels of authority, and relations between captains, vice-captains, and team members, the complex codes through which tactics are communicated, and so on. In the same way, poverty cannot be understood only as the failure of individuals; it must also be understood in the context of the overall distribution of wealth within and between societies by reference to the structure of society.

The example of a professional sports team is an instructive one. The consequence of gradual inflation of the salaries paid to sportspeople at the highest level has meant that fortunes, by any standard, have been earned by a few extremely talented individuals, such as soccer players Lionel Messi or Cristiano Ronaldo. The difficult task for coaches (usually paid a fraction of what their players earn) is to mould these highly paid individuals into a team so that the team's as well as the individual's performance is maximised. Sporting folklore has it that a team of individuals will always beat individuals who make up a team. Sometimes, though, the 'me' concept gets in the way of the 'we' concept. A coach who keeps an expensive player sitting out of the game as a discip-linary measure for failing to maximise team performance is not likely to be popular with the club owners or the fans.

The contrast with the way in which the relationship between the individual and society is constructed in different countries is an instructive one. While in the West there are highly individualised notions of self, in Japanese society, for instance, the relationship between the individual and society is constructed quite differ-ently (see Singer 1993: 96–128; also Mouer and Sugimoto 1986). The primary cultural emphasis on identification with the group means that the relationship between the individual and society is constructed much less as a tension or contradiction than in Western societies where individualism prevails. The individual is considered subservient to the group. The cultural values of loyalty and harmony within the group (family, company, etc.) draw on the traditions of Asian philosophical thought (both Confucian and Buddhist).

This approach to social life, it should be said, also has drawbacks, such as the implications the pursuit of group aims has for the potential harming of outsiders. Many individuals who historically have not conformed to group norms, or who have been discriminated against on the basis of marginalised attributes such as gender, race, and sexuality, have often been persecuted by powerful dominant groups. The important point is that there is nothing inevitable or 'natural' about the nature of group life and the place of the individual within it, rather they are the products of history and culture. The cross-cultural example, however, sheds light on the nature of so-called 'economic individualism', the free-market ideology which holds that individual pursuit of economic gain is the most effective manner to allocate economic resources and that society cannot survive unless individuals aggressively pursue their own individual self-interest. The example of Japan, economically successful by any measure, would seem to be a powerful counter-example.

A simple instance of the consequences of such free-market ideology can be seen in the operation of the housing market, an area which, for most individuals, represents the largest investment made in a lifetime. The market determination of housing prices, based on buying at a lower price and benefiting from a rise in values by selling at a higher price, means that some areas have greater increases than others according to market demand. In some of the larger cities in the world, huge rises in the price of houses have reduced affordability, not only for younger people trying to enter the housing market, but also for many members of occupations on whom the rest of society relies for basic services, such as police, fire, teaching, health, and postal services. Some workers in London have been on strike in an attempt to secure a 'London allowance' (in the form of extra pay) to enable them to afford London housing prices, and thus continue to provide the basic infrastructure of services that the city requires. Such housing pressures are felt in Sydney and Auckland, where house prices greatly exceed those elsewhere in the respective countries. In the Canberra region, many of the workers who provide the basic infrastructure of goods and services that the national capital requires choose, on economic grounds, to live over the New South Wales border in the town of Queanbeyan, where house prices are more affordable.

Another example, outlined previously, is occupational health and safety. For a long time the major form of explanation for the causes of what were called industrial 'accidents' was the notion of 'accident-proneness'. This concept is drawn from industrial Psychology and fails to take into account the broader social causes of what should more properly be called 'industrial injuries'. These social causes include the nature of the work relationship itself, the frequent priority of production over safety considerations, and the lack of adequate safety precautions taken (such as guards on machines). Yet the focus on the individual level without considering the broader group level of analysis effectively blamed the worker for the injuries received (for an extended analysis, see Quinlan and Bohle 1991). Within the field of occupational health and safety is the example of the digging of trenches. Many workers over the years have lost their lives by being buried in collapsing trenches. Digging trenches is a common part of construction work. It is inevitable that, due to soil and climate variations, some trenches will collapse from time to time unless precautions are taken. Cave-ins can thus hardly be called 'accidents' in the sense of unforeseen chance events. Yet the technology for avoiding cave-ins is fairly simple, in the form of shoring, where a steel frame fits down the sides of the trench around where individuals are working and it can be moved by a crane as the workers move along the trench. This costs money, however, including the wages of the crane driver. In all, the personal troubles of being buried in a trench can only be understood at the wider public level of employer–employee relations. Likewise, individual suffering and deprivation of various sorts cannot be understood only as an accumulation of individual experiences, but must also involve locating those individual experiences in their social and structural context – something that is central to a socio-logical way of analysing the social world.

Conclusion

This chapter addressed the question of what is unique about sociological explanation. It is the concern with the relation-ship between the individual and society in a manner seeking to locate the individual in the larger social scheme of things. Furthermore, locating the individual must take account of contradiction and paradox. While there are considerable areas of overlap with other pursuits and other social sciences, the distinct-iveness of a sociological explanation lies in its focus on relating the individual level of social analysis to the collective or group level.

References

AIFS (Australian Institute of Family Studies), 2021. 'Marriage Rates in Australia', Australian Institute of Family Studies, Canberra [https://aifs.gov.au/facts-and-figures/marriage-rates-australia].

Beck, U., and Beck-Gernsheim E., 2002, *Individualization: Institution-alized Individualism and its Social and Political Consequences*. Sage, London.

Berger, P., 1963. *An Invitation to Sociology*. Penguin, New York.

Cave, D., 2020. 'Jacinda Ardern sold a drastic lockdown with straight talk and mom jokes', *New York Times*, 23 May. Updated 7 October, 2020 [www.nytimes.com/2020/05/23/world/asia/jacinda-ardern-coronavirus-new-zealand.html].

Collins, R., 1982, *Sociological Insight: an Introduction to Non-Obvious Sociology*. Oxford University Press, New York.

Durkheim, E., 1970 [1897]. *Suicide: a Study in Sociology*. Routledge and Kegan Paul, London.

Freidson, E., 1986. *Professional Powers: a Study of the Institutionalisation of Formal Knowledge*, University of Chicago Press, Chicago.

Goldthorpe, J.C., 1974. *An Introduction to Sociology*. Cambridge University Press, London.

Mouer, R., and Sugimoto, Y., 1986. *Images of Japanese Society: a Study in the Social Construction of Reality*. KPI, London.

New Daily (newspaper), 2021. 'No COVID suicide epidemic', 18 April [https://thenewdaily.com.au/life/wellbeing/2021/04/18/no-covid-suicide-epidemic/].

New Statesman, 2020. 'The suicide epidemic among Northern Ireland's "Ceasefire Babies"', 14 January [www.newstatesman.com/politics/2020/01/suicide-epidemic-among-northern-ireland-s-ceasefire-babies].

New York Times (newspaper), 2020. 'Sinking in Venice' [www.nytimes.com/2000/09/12/science/l-sinking-in-venice-109800.html].

O'Malley, P., 1975. 'Suicide and War', *British Journal of Criminology*, 15:4, 348–359.

O'Neill, J., 2009. *The Irish Potato Famine*. ABDO, Minnesota.

Quinlan, M., and Bohle, P., 1991. *Managing Occupational Health and Safety in Australia: a Multidisciplinary Approach*. Macmillan, South Melbourne.

Rosenberg, A., 2016. *Philosophy of Social Science*. Routledge. London.

Singer, P., 1993. *How Are We to Live? Ethics in an Age of Self-Interest*. Text Publishing, Melbourne.

Smith-Rosenberg, C., and Rosenberg, C., 1973. 'The Female Animal: Medical and Biological Views of Woman and Her Role in Nineteenth Century America', *Journal of American History*, 60:2, 332–356.

Thatcher, M., 2013. 'Margaret Thatcher: a life in quotes', *Guardian*, 8 April [www.theguardian.com/politics/2013/apr/08/margaret-thatcher-quotes].

UNICEF (United Nations International Children's Emergency Fund), 1994. *State of the World's Children*. UNICEF, New York.

Urry, J., 1990. *The Tourist Gaze: Leisure and Travel in Contemporary Societies*. Sage, London.

4 The sociological imagination

The basic concepts outlined earlier are important to all Sociologists: the distinction between sociological and social problems, between macro and micro Sociology, between private troubles and public issues, between continuity and change, and the importance of reflexivity. How most Sociologists work with these basic sociological ideas is to pursue the answers to a number of key questions. These questions are: *What's happening? Why? What are the consequences? How do you know? How could it be otherwise?* The early Sociologists, amongst them Durkheim, Marx, and Weber, began to explore these concepts and questions and apply them to the societies in which they lived. Sociologists continue this project to this day, moulding and adapting these basic concepts and questions to their own version of Sociology and to their ever-changing worlds.

As we have seen, one sociologist whose version of these questions has been particularly influential is C. Wright Mills. Writing in 1959, he gathered together these questions and concepts and labelled the perspective that uses them to view the world, 'the sociological imagination'. Our interpretation of this perspective is that the quest for sociological understanding of the world involves invoking the sociological imagination as a form of consciousness for understanding social processes. Here, and in the following chapters, this notion is developed in some detail by arguing for a number of sensibilities or components to the sociological imagination. *Sensibility*, in this instance, means a keen appreciation of, or consciousness about, aspects of explanation.

DOI: 10.4324/9781003316329-4

Our starting point is with the work of the British sociologist Anthony Giddens (1983: 16), who interprets the sociological imagination as 'several related forms of sensibility indispensable to sociological analysis'. For him, the sociological quest for 'an understanding of the social world initiated by the contemporary industrial societies' can only be achieved by the exercise of these forms of sociological imagination. For Giddens, the exercise is threefold: historical, cultural, and critical. To this schema we shall add a fourth dimension, that of structure. Sociological explanation is likely to be incomplete unless these four considerations are taken into account. This chapter will deal with the historical and cultural aspects, the next chapter with the structural and critical.

Historical

Giddens (1983) argued that one consequence of the attempt to model Sociology on the natural sciences and to uncover general laws of human behaviour has been the severing of Sociology from history as the social processes have been isolated from their historical context. But the two are so closely intertwined as to be virtually indistinguishable. As Giddens (1983: 165–166) says:

> We have to grasp how history is made through the active involvements and struggles of human beings, and yet at the same time both forms those human beings and produces outcomes which they neither intend nor foresee. As a theoretical background to the social sciences, nothing is more vital.

In other words, because history has an enormous effect on who we are as individuals and societies, it must be integral to the study of Sociology. Wright Mills (1959) has alternatively characterised the relationship between the individual and society as between biography and history, as well as the way these intersect within social structures. Where does this particular individual stand as part of this particular society in relation to history? Where do individuals, such as Barack Obama, Donald Trump, Diego Maradona, or Queen Elizabeth II, stand in relation to their particular societies at this point in history? Like the discipline of history, Sociology also attempts to gain some understanding and comprehension of societies that no longer exist. The origins of Sociology lie in the attempt to come to terms with and understand the massive transformation in the social world that we generally call the advent of modernity. Arguably, the ongoing social changes that have occurred in the past two centuries are more profound and far-reaching than any that occurred over the previous 10,000 years.

Some Sociologists argue that the pace of social change has accelerated in recent decades, so that the state of society is now sufficiently different from that of even our parents; we live in a distinguishably new period of human history. We have moved from the period of modernity to that of *postmodernity*, characterised by forms of social life and institutions that change dynamically. The nature of such change has been described by Bauman (2000) as 'liquid modernity'. These changes include a lack of permanence in people's lives as the old certainties by which people lived dissolve. While there was always a significant minority who were exceptions, these 'certainties' about the bulk of one's life included being married to one person, living in the same house for long periods, having a relatively fixed identity, and having long-term employment in one job. With this new period of insecurity has come the end of the notion of global narratives such as 'progress' as well as faith in the ability of science and technology to solve the problems we face (for a review of the debate see Turner 1997). Other Sociologists argue, by contrast, that while there have been major changes in how people live their lives, these changes have not been so monumental as to justify designating a new historical epoch. Instead, there is enough similarity with previous times to justify the term 'late modernity' (see Giddens 1991).

Coming to terms with these changes requires a clear understanding of the historical aspects, the first element in a sociological imagination. Attempts to understand particular social phenomena, even current social phenomena, are likely to be inadequate unless the historical aspects are considered. As far back as the late 1890s Emile Durkheim set out how important history is for Sociology when he stated:

> One doesn't know social reality if one only sees it from out-
> side and if one ignores the sub-structure. In order to know
> how it is, it is necessary to know how it has come to be, that
> is, to have followed in history the manner in which it has
> been progressively formed. In order to be able to say with
> any chance of success what the society of tomorrow will
> be …, it is indispensable to have studied the social forms of
> the most distant past. In order to understand the present it is
> necessary to go outside of it.
>
> (Cited in Bellah 1959)

The importance of an historical sensibility goes to the heart
of the sociological perspective and the sociological imagination
because it allows us to see how change occurs through which
institutional and group based processes. All three of Sociology's
acknowledged founders and major theorists, Karl Marx, Max
Weber, and Emile Durkheim produced theories about the social
world that are deeply historical in orientation. Their attempts to
describe and understand the institutional bases of the profound
changes to the social and economic conditions of Europe, and
related consequences on institutional development and social
relationships, is drawn from comparisons with conditions from
previous ages. It wasn't really possible for these early Sociologists
to express their ideas about social change without an historical
sensibility because the modernity they aimed to describe and
understand was in various complex ways a product of the social
processes of what proceeded it.

Marx and Weber notably drew deeply on a comparative historical method in their analyses of modernity. Marx (1988
[1932]) promoted a central theory of social and economic
change broadly called 'historical materialism', which aimed to
show how society 'evolves' and changes through key elements
of 'the material conditions of life' such as the production process (including technology and human labour) and its impacts
on social relations between classes, or relations to production,
in arriving at the modern world. For Marx the stages of society
are characterised by what he called 'modes of production', that
is, how an economy produces goods and services. For example,

Marx considers such modes as the Ancient (agrarianism of Classical Greece and Rome), the Feudal (farm estates of Medieval Europe), and the Capitalist (Industrial production). Each mode was defined by certain technologies and forces that shaped the social world of the time and led to the development of the next mode. In this way Marx attempted to explain not only the nature of social relationships in various material circumstances as a result of each mode of production, but under what conditions and how they had changed.

Weber's theory on the origins of capitalism (2002) is characterised by comparative analyses of numerous historical societies such as ancient Israel, ancient China, and ancient India, as well the cultural and economic conditions in Europe in the seventeenth century. Weber was interested in what was unique about Western Europe, which, for him, produced the institutional and cultural seedbed for the development of a specific kind of capitalism that is central to the modern world economy. Why did a certain kind of capitalism originate in Europe at a certain time? This question led Weber to consider a range of historical, social, and cultural 'conditions' such as the impact of religion, the family, and types of government or authority that acted as levers constraining or releasing certain kinds of cultural and economic progress.

History is a central concern for Sociology, yet the way Sociologists use historical evidence as part of the sociological imagination is somewhat different from the way it is used by many conventional historians. While it is difficult to generalise, many mainstream historians attempt to understand the past for its own sake. Engaging in historical research is often pursued as an end in itself. In Sociology, the quest is to understand the present in terms of how it came to be. The past is studied not just for its own sake but for what it can tell us about the shape our current society takes. To understand some aspect of our society, we first need to study the past. The 'facts' of what happened in the past are as important to Sociologists as they are to conventional historians, but the use made of these facts is more often put in an interpretive context. All scholarship involves selectivity, and what facts are selected as relevant will depend on the purpose for which the research is being conducted. Sociologists more often consider the implications of these facts for modern-day life. For example, where Marx focused on the changing material conditions structuring changing social relations, Weber's approach emphasised the role of culture on economic and social change leading to modernity. Marx and Weber's diverse uses of history in their explanations of modern society is one of the very interesting sociological debates concerning the making of the modern world. Weber accepted a lot of what Marx had to say about the role of material conditions in the development of the modern socio-economic system but suggested that cultural elements such as religion were important behavioural catalysts for changes in economic activity.

In this sense, historical sensibility is the background to all understanding if it is not to be what is called *ahistorical*. This term means failing to understand and take account of the historical context in explaining what has occurred. Durkheim's work is often seen as ahistorical by many Sociologists; however, Bellah (1959) and others suggest that his work is in fact deeply historical and an historical sensibility has impacted a wide range of Durkheim's studies in Sociology, especially relating to the family and religion.

An example of an ahistorical approach is often associated with certain views about poverty. A prevailing sentiment about economic disadvantage is that many people who are in poverty or chronic financial distress only have themselves to blame. That despite perhaps some lean patches in recent times, if you want to work and succeed you will; it's just up to you. This sentiment is shared by many like-minded individuals but also seems to underscore some forms of recent neo-liberal social policy. Despite perhaps some aspects of this mantra being possible for a minority, there is a lot about the nature and experience of poverty that this sentiment misses. Firstly, poverty is a complex condition often relating to a variety of powerful seen and unseen factors beyond the control of the individual, such as availability of work, kinds of work one can access, and educational opportunities where one lives. Second, and most importantly for our purposes, a focus on individualism as the locus of economic success or failure, is ahistorical and incomplete. Poverty is often inherited and reproduced from earlier social and economic conditions within the context of the family and community. An individual is born into a set of circumstances, which is very much like a lottery. What we have learned from the sociological perspective is that if you are lucky enough to be born into a wealthy family then you are more than likely to be wealthy yourself later in life and vice versa. This is due to the various economic and social supports and opportunities, not to mention less tangible benefits such as esteem and confidence derived from favourable economic conditions.

Economic inequality hasn't changed drastically in many societies in over three hundred years according to French economist Thomas Piketty (2014). Social class often heavily determines various future economic, cultural, and social opportunities such as education, social networks, health, and leisure for most people. The same logic pervades the chronic social disadvantage of many marginalised social groups such as First Nations peoples, people of colour in the global north, women, and migrants, whose histories are replete with forms of oppression and exclusion deeply impacting on their present conditions. A clear aim of much social policy – where Sociology often has made strong contributions through identifying the causes of social problems – is to attempt to redress the historical record for the marginalised. This is achieved in part with forms of state-based support to enable people to experience what Sociologists call *social mobility*, that is, the movement out of poverty and into some fraction of the working or middle classes.

Another example of the importance of an historical sensibility when it comes to the sociological imagination is crime. Crime and deviance have forever been fascinating subjects for Sociologists and Sociology students alike. Crime defines the boundaries of society, that is, what is acceptable behaviour and what isn't for groups and communities. Most behaviour that is defined as criminal we would consider to be fairly intuitive, such as theft, violent assault, and murder under most circumstances; that has been the case in many societies and cultures throughout history. However, there are many forms of human behaviour that, for various reasons, have been defined as deviant or criminal, which in turn have come to be considered acceptable and lawful over time. In understanding how crime and deviance change, and indeed how this aspect of society is socially constructed, we need to invoke an historical sensibility.

Many countries have law reform movements that aim to make the laws of the land more just and the legal process more efficient and accessible. But legislative change determining what a crime is or isn't, is often a reflection or consequence of social change. For example, homosexual activity has only recently been decriminalised in many countries (despite remaining a crime still in many others). Further, it's only very recently that, again in some countries, gay and lesbian couples can marry like anyone else. Prohibitions and persecutions against homosexual activity have historically been long held, and derive mostly from moral codes associated with the major religious faiths and ecclesiastical courts that then passed into the common law in countries such as the United Kingdom. A combination of declining religious influence, gay and lesbian social movements, and increased tolerance of difference, created the social conditions for the laws to change.

In some places, up until recently, going to see a psychic or 'soothsayer' was a criminal offence also. In the state of Victoria in Australia, it technically still is a crime (at the time of writing) under the Vagrancy Act (1964). Some laws (and by association crimes), are simply outdated, others are the subject of major social change where crime and justice are historically lagging behind social progress. Most behaviour defined as criminal, however, will have an historical basis either in a cultural setting such as religious doctrine, the common law (as in the British tradition), or in other political or state-based domination. For example, the various Christian Churches have had considerable political and legal influence in many societies and have brought that influence to bear on behaviour such as consulting 'soothsayers' and psychics. Seeing a psychic or magician (a common practice throughout history) has been an ancient transgression for a practising Christian. Historically this relates to how organised religion and magic have been powerful social influences and in some respects in competition for souls (Thomas 1971) in the construction of meaning. However, with the decline in social influence of Christianity the 'crime' of consulting a psychic has lost importance and social stigma.

Social media provides an interesting contemporary example of an historical process in action. Much like shady soothsayers, 'influencers' and other self-styled authorities that spread fake news or misinformation on certain topics are in the early stages of being prosecuted or at least restricted by the authorities and controllers of social media. The law on these matters is still being worked out, but in the future, we will look back on the historical development of the social use of the internet and the forms of mass communication it has engendered and consider it in relation to the various crimes that have emerged from its misuse as a measure of social change.

Another interesting example is the criminalising and decriminalising of drug use. For many centuries illicit/narcotic substances were used regularly for everyday and also religious purposes (many Christians still partake in alcohol as part of the Eucharist). It wasn't until modern times that such substances were altogether banned or made illegal (with the occasional exception of alcohol). Religious cultural moorings no longer circumscribe drug use in many societies. Enormous problems with uncontrolled abuse of certain substances, including legal substances such as alcohol prevail, causing seemingly intractable social problems. The general response from law makers in many societies (such as the 'war on drugs') has been to heavily criminalise drug use, yet getting tough on crime through harsh sentencing and other measures hasn't proven to be much of a solution to the crimes associated with drug abuse, or as a deterrent to continued substance use.

The evaluative history of such penalties has been to drive drugs 'underground' creating a raft of further associated problems and criminal activity without any decrease in drug abuse. Billions of dollars of public money, rising organised crime, increased stigmatisation for those addicted, and government and agency corruption are just some of the features of heavily criminalising substance abuse, exacerbating already difficult problems. One response to the historical failures of criminalising drug abuse has been to shift the emphasis from crime to health, so that addiction becomes not a crime, but a health issue. Of course, drug trafficking is a different matter. Defined with the emphasis on health, that is, as an illness, drug addiction can be treated, with some hope that the affected can resume a normal life far better than if they were convicted as a criminal, and at the same time save lives and reduce the huge amounts of public spending on law enforcement. The Portuguese government decriminalised all drug use and possession in 2001 and as a result have severely reduced numbers of drug related crimes, cases of HIV, and drug related deaths (*Guardian* 2017). Portugal has taken a different historical route on drugs than most countries with some stunning success.

Another example of the importance of an historical sensibility might be the current culturally approved body shape, particularly for women, but also for men. A walk through any art gallery shows that the current fashionable body shape with its emphasis on slenderness is only of recent origin. Art gallery walls are adorned with paintings of fuller, hourglass figures for women (painted by artists such as Botticelli) – figures once considered beautiful but now considered fat. Body shaping is now a massive industry in many countries; indeed one of the features of late modernity is claimed to be that the body has become a project to be worked on rather than something to have or occupy (see Shilling 2003). It is worked on by dieting, surgical alterations, injections, implants, hair dyeing, shaving, waxing, piercing, plucking, tattooing, building up, exercising, and so on. All are designed to achieve a figure that is currently defined as fashionable and beautiful. An historical perspective on body shapes is therefore important. It allows us to challenge the belief that what is currently fashionable, including slimness, is somehow more 'natural'.

An historical awareness also helps us to make sense of new developments in the way our society is organised and is fundamental to the sociological quest, serving not just classical theories, but also informs a number of crucial contemporary theoretical developments in Sociology such as feminism, studies in sexual identities, and ethnic and racial studies. Employing an historical sensibility here elucidates the social conditions and processes under which women, gays and lesbians, people of colour, and First Nations people have been made marginal, and in turn produces a reflexive orientation to social problems, leading to a discourse about how social change is possible. Such contemporary movements as Black Lives Matter, Women's March, and the many forms of activism on behalf of various sexual identity groups, relate the historical and contemporary social positions of individuals and groups who claim these identities. For many, identity is the partaking in or belonging to more than one such group. The compounding effects of being a person of colour and female, for example, in many places throughout history have given rise to emerging patterns made clear by the sociological imagination. In Sociology the awareness of how these identity factors are interrelated is called *intersectionality*.

Cultural

The second component of a sociological imagination is a sensibility to the cultural aspects of explanation. *Culture* is one of the central concepts of the discipline of Sociology, as it is for anthropology. In these disciplines, however, the term 'culture' is not used in its conventional sense as something equivalent to civilisation or the 'higher' forms of artistic expression, such as classical music and opera (although these forms are the subject of some rather interesting sociological studies – see below). Rather, it is used to refer to the non-biological aspects of society, all those things which are learnt or are symbolic, including convention, custom, and language. Together these components distinguish human behaviour and society from that of other primates.

Culture includes such features as beliefs, values, ways of life, and customary ways of doing things. The scholarly discipline that takes the concept of culture as its central organising principle is anthropology; not only in its more traditional form of the study of non-Western traditional societies but also, most recently, in its focus on aspects of industrial and post-industrial society. Yet a cultural sensitivity has also been a feature of the sociological imagination since the earliest days of the discipline of Sociology. The cultivation of cultural insights is important to the quest for a sociological understanding for two main reasons. One is to push back what is frequently the conventionally held notion of the boundary between the natural and the social world. The other is to challenge notions that some cultures are superior to others.

The question of the boundary between the natural and the social world is of major intellectual importance. Some disciplines, such as Psychology, devote much of their energy to elucidating this boundary. The particular importance of a cultural perspective is to reveal, as several decades of anthropological research has done, the range and diversity of the means of human existence that have been followed in human societies, such that it is difficult with any certainty to say what is 'natural' or 'normal' for human society. Rather, we can talk about culturally specific forms that particular societies adopt. An example is mate selection.

In Western society, monogamy (the coupling of one woman with one man) is the conventional social arrangement under which reproduction occurs. Yet anthropological evidence shows that virtually any combination of partners you can think of in terms of numbers of men and women are to be found in other societies (see Burns et al. 1983). To say that monogamy is the natural social arrangement is clearly nonsociological. Likewise, the current cultural pattern for mate selection in many places is through 'love marriages', a supposedly free choice of partners. Yet as Reeves (2014) has argued, Cupid's arrows are often carefully aimed with the help of parents through such strategies as selection of schools and the encouragement of certain leisure activities. Many other cultures favour arranged marriages, where parents select the mate, usually on the grounds of some perceived compatibility. One system is not more natural than the other, nor should it be assumed that love marriages are superior to arranged marriages – the divorce rate attests to that fallacy.

It is this debunking of commonsense understandings of how society works that has been the role of traditional anthropology. One influential American anthropologist, Margaret Mead (1901–78), lived in Samoa during 1925–26, where she studied and wrote a controversial work (published in 1930) about the experience of growing up in that society, especially for young women. Her purpose was to hold up a mirror to North American society of the time. This society was, in her view, obsessed with the 'problems' of that span of the life cycle called 'adolescence' or 'youth'. In her mirror, she hoped Americans might see their own concerns reflected. Understanding how very differently Samoan young people experienced that span of the life cycle brought into question much of the way in which the debates about young people in the United States were couched in terms of what was 'natural' or not.

Along with an awareness of the variety of forms of human organisation possible is the second component of a cultural sensibility – the dispelling of what is called *ethnocentrism*. The quest for a sociological understanding involves the task of overcoming a position that assumes one's own culture is superior to others and the standard against which others should be measured. *Racism*, the belief that one's own race or ethnic group is superior to others, is the most common expression of ethnocentrism. Of course, both racism and ethnocentrism have been potent forces in shaping world history. Their legacy has been slavery, genocide, ethnic cleansing, and apartheid. Indeed, some of the worst atrocities have been perpetrated by one set of people against others on the basis of a claim that the race of the oppressors was superior. As Giddens (1983: 23) argues, ethnocentrism is deeply entrenched in Western culture, though it is also found in many (if not most) other cultures. He argues it is a challenge to:

> break away from the belief, implicit or explicit, that the modes of life which have developed in the West are somehow superior to those of other cultures. Such a belief is encouraged by the very spread of Western capitalism itself, which has set in motion a train of events that has corroded or destroyed most other cultures with which it has come into contact.

An interesting example of debunking the notion of naturalness leading to ethnocentrism is found in the work of Norbert Elias. Elias (1978) turned the sociological imagination to many topics, but his major contribution was a unique theory of social interaction through analyses of changes in emotions, manners, and etiquette over a long historical period. In his classic work, *The Civilizing Process*, Elias was interested in how most everyday social interaction had become a fairly constrained and passive set of rituals between individuals of different social groups, especially between social classes. The 'civilising process' was the term he gave to a series of historical behavioural patterns that attempted to explain the self-applied notion of 'civilised' to European societies such as Germany, France, and England.

He contrasts emotional expression between individuals and groups, and attitudes towards the body from around the twelfth century to the early twentieth. He does this via analyses of etiquette books, whose contents demonstrate distinct changes in the direction of the management of the emotions and the body towards 'civility' or increasing restraint, through the centuries. For example, Elias describes how people in the middle ages were far less emotionally reserved than people in the early twentieth century, citing how even friends might meet in the street and be laughing one minute but be involved in a serious affray with swords the next. He also cites various instructions for not urinating, defecating, or spitting at the dinner table, showing one's private parts, and speaking in the manner of a 'yokel'. Of course in showing that these behaviours are at one point in time discouraged and forbidden through an instructional guide to manners, he is demonstrating that a social process and not a natural one is at the heart of behavioural change. Many of the behaviours he cites as selected for sanction in the etiquette books seem entirely natural to be sequestered to our current sensibilities, such as urinating or even defecating at a table (toilets are a somewhat modern invention) but were seemingly tolerated behaviours for Europeans up until relatively recently.

His sociological explanation for the 'civilising process' resulting in the changes in manners and emotions was that various social groups became more and more dependent on each other as political and economic power became increasingly concentrated in the hands of a monarchy or noble family. This occurs to the point where modern society, as defined by an entity such as a large nation state, oversees most of how an individual lives and determines the cultural expectations of behaviour (what

Elias terms a 'threshold') and enforces the laws when they are transgressed. This is in contrast to medieval societies in Europe, which were a series of mostly separate and much smaller political regions such as a duchy, and where nobles were literally a law unto themselves. Elias debunks the notion that Europeans are innately 'civilised', as etiquette is entirely invented and learned through a system of social relations as a means of deference to, and a symbol of, power. The notion of seeing oneself as 'civilised' through behavioural standards has been important in Europeans viewing other cultures as inferior and has served as a rationale for colonisation, slavery, and oppression summed up in notions such as the 'white man's burden' (Kipling [1899] 2018).

Avoiding ethnocentrism in the quest for sociological understanding involves an awareness of *cultural relativity* – that cultures do not exist on a hierarchy from better to worse. Rather, cultures are different so one cannot judge the cultural practices of other cultures by one's own notions of what is appropriate behaviour. What can seem a normal practice in one country can seem very unusual in another. A nice example is Dutch windows. In Anglo-Celtic culture, notions of privacy and the distinction between public and private space are such that at nightfall it is usually considered culturally appropriate to draw the curtains or blinds over domestic windows; in other words, to mark off what occurs within the living spaces of private dwellings as private in the sense of removed from public gaze. A visitor to the Netherlands is therefore likely to be struck by the observance of a different cultural tradition, that of leaving downstairs windows uncovered at dusk to permit, indeed even encourage passers-by to observe the, most often, beautifully decorated interiors as well as families going about their daily lives (see Vera 1989). Indeed a visitor is likely to feel somewhat uncomfortable (something akin to a peeping Tom) at observing these rituals of daily life that are considered private in other cultures.

From the point of view of many Asians, the cultural practice in most Western households of wearing shoes inside domestic dwellings is inappropriate on the grounds of cleanliness and hygiene. Likewise, the response to hot summer temperatures in this part of the world is to strip off to shorts and brief swimming costumes. In Arab countries, the response is to cover up, including head covers. In the light of concerns about the increasing rates of skin cancers, it is difficult to avoid the conclusion that the latter response is more appropriate. A woman of Filipino ethnic background lives in the same suburb as one of the authors. She wears a pendant around her neck, which is very precious to her. It was made from her grandfather's thighbone. Some locals have referred to this practice as 'bizarre'. We often have no difficulty labelling customs in other cultures pejoratively but have difficulty recognising the same in our own. The wearing of lucky charms in other cultures might be dismissed as superstitious, yet some aspects of custom in our own might also be considered to have the status of lucky charms. One is the common sight of cyclists riding along with their protective bike helmets not on their heads, but strung over the handlebars. Beliefs in its powers as a lucky charm to keep the cyclist safe seems the obvious explanation! Another is the practice of hanging St Christopher icons from car rear-vision mirrors, an attempt to ward off accidents, even by some considerably lapsed or non-Catholics. A cultural sensibility would recognise that a St Christopher pendant is no more 'civilised' or 'natural' than the thighbone of a loved one.

At the same time, questioning the limits to cultural relativity is important and very much part of exercising a sociological imagination through a cultural sensibility. On these grounds it may be necessary and indeed appropriate to argue that some things that other people do cannot be legitimatised on the grounds of cultural relativity. An example is the different positions occupied by women cross-culturally. Some cultures are what we call highly *patriarchal*, that is, they experience a system of power relations organised in such a manner that men benefit the most. In some places, the position of women, who are exploited and repressed, is legitimatised by major belief systems and legal codes. In some countries in the Middle East, up until very recently, women were not allowed by law to hold a driver's licence.

An issue debated often in recent years is the cultural practice of 'circumcising' baby girls, which continues to be done by some migrants, particularly those of African origin, even after their arrival in countries such as the United Kingdom and Australia.

The practice involves the removal of parts of the external genitals, especially the clitoris. Its purpose is reported to be the control of female sexuality, since the operation allegedly deadens sexual sensation and therefore is supposed to make the women less tempted into extramarital sexual relationships (see Armstrong 1991). The issue is the degree to which cultural relativity should be extended before the practice is defined as 'mutilation', or an 'assault', and therefore incorporated under the definition of 'child abuse'. If defined as child abuse, should it warrant the attention of policing authorities and child protection legislation (see Family Law Council 1994)? The question has increasingly been cast in a human rights language framework or *discourse*: are there fundamental human rights (such as not having genitals 'altered') which override cultural expectations? Are human rights absolute or culturally relative?

Yet even in this instance where condemnation has been widespread, issues of cultural sensitivity and relativity are relevant, particularly in deciding how best to bring about the cessation of the practice. If female genital mutilation is the answer, what is the question? Are there alternate, more socially acceptable means of answering that question? For one thing, it must be seen in the context of social pressure on mothers to conform to cultural expectations to help assure their daughter's future marriageability. We might then seek to address other, more acceptable means of bringing about a desired end result. If condemning such a practice outright, perhaps it is also necessary to consider cultural practices in the wider community, for instance, that of male circumcision. If removing part of the genitalia of baby girls is mutilation, why does the same standard not apply to removal of part of the genitalia of baby boys? There is similarly no medical justification. Yet attempts to have the surgical procedure 'chopped off' the list of operations for which part of the payment to surgeons is claimable from the public purse (on the grounds that it was a type of cosmetic surgery) led to a public outcry and a hasty backdown by the Australian Government. Furthermore, an historical sensitivity is also important. It is perhaps not widely known that clitoridectomies (the operation to remove the clitoris) were performed on adult women psychiatric patients in the nineteenth and early twentieth centuries in developed countries such as the United States (Barker-Benfield 1972). The purpose of the procedure then was also to make the women more 'manageable'. From a particular moral point of view, condemnation may be right and proper, but a cultural sensitivity arising out of a sense of cultural relativity is also important to the sociological imagination.

A sensitivity to cultural difference is a crucial component of the sociological imagination. Cultural difference can operate at a number of levels. The usual commonsense understanding is the *intersocietal* level; that is, between different societies. Here the effect of a sociological imagination can be powerful. It can introduce a new level of understanding about aspects of our society that are assumed to be a natural part of the human condition but which are, in fact, culturally constructed. A poignant example is religion. In recent times the role of religion in global culture and politics has been acutely emphasised as a key factor in various international and intrasocietal conflicts and disputes. A common opinion suggested the rise of religious violence in some places was attributable to the key tenets of a religion such as Islam, fuelling suspicion on all Muslims as being prone to religiously inspired violence. The truth is that major global faiths such as Islam are highly culturally complex, diverse, and nonviolent. Islam is practised all over the world and is the major or official faith in over 20 countries, with around 1.8 billion adherents stretching from Saudi Arabia to Indonesia (Pew Research Centre 2017).

Culturally there are many different manifestations of how Islam is interpreted, practised, and applied, yet all claim to be Islamic. In some countries where Islam is the majority religion, such as Saudi Arabia, social and cultural conditions are very strict, but in others, such as Indonesia, they can be quite liberal. For example, popular cultural events in Indonesia (Java especially) are drag queen singing contests. Performers' feminine personas are inspired by international pop stars, complete with soulful renditions of their songs, but performers also sing traditional folk music such as 'dangdut'. Many of the performers are observant Muslims who refrain from alcohol (*Vogue* 2017). While the performances are largely tolerated and celebrated, government religious authorities do from time to time seek to cancel the contests on religious grounds, after which strong public protests have ensued. In one such protest a banner read that Indonesians were as pious as anyone else, but also related 'we are not the United States, but neither are we Saudi Arabia'. Religious faiths such as Islam do promote central teachings and practices, but just what these are, how these are interpreted and applied, and in what areas of life, are often very diverse, inconsistent, and subject to continual interpretation based on distinct intersocietal cultural differences.

The same logic of cultural differences and diverse religious realities holds for the other major world faiths, where a religion's teachings and practices are subject to the cultural histories and conditions of the societies in which they are given life. Another example is some of Haydn's research, which investigated Western conversion to Buddhism (Phillips and Aarons 2005; 2007). In a globalised world where cultural traffic is exchanged rapidly through electronic communication, travel, and publishing, many Westerners have taken up serious interest in the religions of Asia, such as Buddhism. How Buddhism is interpreted and practised in countries like the United States, Australia, and the United Kingdom by these adherents is often at serious odds with how Buddhism is lived in its traditional historical settings such as Thailand, Sri Lanka, Cambodia, and Japan. For a start, some adherence to Buddhism is, in its more traditional settings, often a form of family obligation for many young men, who enter a monastery for a year of two to gain merit for a favourable rebirth for one's parents. Buddhist monasteries can be quite powerful institutions in these countries and have some political sway. Often there is some resentment on the part of youths, who have to enter a celibate and highly restrictive lifestyle for a key time in their young lives; however, the cultural and familial obligations are strong.

In the West, Buddhist monasteries are few, and opportunities to learn and develop one's practice limited. Buddhism in the West is often an amalgam of various different traditions, sometimes patched together by various teachers and scholars, because the historical religious institutions such as monasteries do not exist to support its development. Adherents in the West adopt and adapt Buddhist teachings and practices as best they can around the cultural and social conditions present. Cultural differences concerning religion continue unabated in the modern West, with many combining some aspects of Buddhism with other spiritual and religious elements in forming some kind of spiritual identity, the process of which has been referred to as shopping in the 'spiritual marketplace' (Roof 2001). In socio-logical terms, what is occurring is that the meaning of religion is socially constructed in different ways in different cultures. Buddhism or Islam in one country has a range of meanings, while in other countries these religions are interpreted and practised differently with a series of quite different meanings. No meaning or interpretation of a religious tradition is more 'natural' or 'normal' than another, and behavioural tendencies such as violence or compassion cannot be reduced to some form of 'natural state' such as core teachings.

At the intersocietal level (between societies), cultural differences are important in explaining how different societies develop. This can occur at either a micro level, involving some small aspect of the society, or at the macro level, between societies as a whole. With various forms of social division being such a large feature of the modern world, a sensitivity to cultural difference is important to the sociological imagination within societies at the *intrasocietal* level (within the same society). One example of intrasocietal cultural difference is the cultural taste espoused by members of different social classes. Cultural taste is the subject of much recent Sociology wherein tastes mark pronounced cultural boundaries between social classes leading to various forms of social and eco-nomic inequality. Many Sociologists are very interested in how people practise or display culture, from their musical tastes and fashion choices, to what kinds of car they drive and their choice of media for news and entertainment. Much of this research follows the work of the French sociologist Pierre Bourdieu, who wrote a famous book on this topic in the late 1970s – *Distinction: a Social Critique of the Judgement of Taste* (Bourdieu 1984 [1979]). In this work, Bourdieu's key argument is that the culture one likes is the product of social position and that 'having taste', or 'being classy', is not the result of innate qualities relating to the appreciation of beauty but of a long and deliberate process of cultivation and socialisation where people whose families have the resources can and do socialise them into developing knowledge around 'legitimate' culture. In Bourdieu's analysis, cultural artefacts such as classical music, types of art, and 'serious' literature are important and others less so, because of a complex system of patronage and privilege. As these forms of art and culture become consecrated through national institutions and are emphasised in schools, they are recognised officially as 'culture' and gain a certain currency as 'legitimate'.

Having competence with 'legitimate' culture such as appreciating classical music, or having read and understood Shakespeare, is attaining what Bourdieu calls 'cultural capital'. Certain socially structured cultural differences between Bach and Brittany Spears, or between Botticelli and Banksy, for Bourdieu, are not necessarily attributed to their respective talents, although differences in quality exist, but how they are elevated or devalued by society and represent cultural difference is a social process within a given society. For example, Shakespeare hasn't always been considered canonical (Smith 2010); in fact some of his plays were considered to be the equivalent of a sixteenth century sitcom, in that they had large popular appeal and weren't seen as intellectually challenging as some of his other works. You can sense the social impact of cultural differences at an intrasocietal level with an experiment. Assess certain playlists you might have. How might the music on these playlists be similar and different from the music of others such as your friends or parents? Would you be comfortable having this playlist made available publically to your friends, or would there be a cringe moment or two as some of your musical guilty pleasures are revealed? Would you be considered as someone without taste, a hipster, a try-hard, or something more neutral because of your choices in music? Follow up with a question to yourself about how you came to like the music you do, and what influence your friends, family, school, and others have had on your tastes. From music you can sociologically analyse other taste choices such as clothes or hairstyles, tattoos or piercings.

A final example is the recycling of water. In the era of climate change, with global warming and the drying of the climate in many parts of the world, water is becoming a more precious resource than ever before. Thus, culturally, we are beginning to value water more. There are observable cultural changes. Firstly there is the minimisation of water usage through such practices as installing dual flush toilets and water efficient shower heads, personal hygiene practices (e.g. having the tap off while brushing teeth), waterless public urinals, composting toilets, and following the adage in relation to toilet flushing 'if it's yellow let it mellow; if it's brown flush it down'! Another move is towards the recycling and reuse of water; separation into grey water that can be used again and black water that cannot. In many societies this shortage has led to recycled water being put back into the drinking supply after treatment. Many cities are now heavily dependent on recycled water for the domestic water supply of its citizens. London is one of the leading cities in the world; by the time Londoners pour themselves a glass of tap water it is estimated to have already been through the kidneys of six or seven others (*Guardian* 2013)! Yet suggestions that it occurs in countries such as Australia have been firmly rejected. A referendum in 2006, in the Queensland regional city of Toowoomba, rejected a plan to introduce a portion of recycled water into the town supply with a vote of 62 per cent against the water plan. A key feature of the rejection of recycled drinking water was what is called the 'yuck factor', a somewhat childish cultural disdain for the prospect of drinking water that has been passed through others (*Brisbane Courier Mail* 2006).

At the same time, talking about the culture of a society is not to assume that everyone in a particular society shares a particular culture. Indeed, Sociologists have found it useful to talk about the idea of *dominant cultures* and *subcultures*, which to some extent relates to our example of cultural taste earlier. However, there are other forms of dominant cultures and subcultures. For example, male dominance or patriarchy has been, to a greater or lesser extent, an aspect of the dominant culture in many societies. But it is a dominance of heterosexual preference. Homosexual men have constituted a significant subculture in many societies.

Likewise, cultural expectations are not uniformly adhered to. Gender is a good example here. Different forms of femininity and masculinity, which have been subsumed under dominant modes of gendered behaviour, are emerging. How people are gendered is changing due to changing cultural expectations. We can see this quite clearly with respects to women, but also with men, especially in areas such as work and family, but also in forms of self-identity, where gender fluidity and queerness challenge the various cultural norms of what men and women, boys and girls are. The adoption and support of personal pronouns, such as he/him, she/her, they/their illustrate this.

Historical and cultural considerations together

A sensibility to and awareness of both historical and cultural aspects is important in a practical respect for the sociological imagination as it enables us to understand societies for their uniqueness. An historical and cultural sensitivity, furthermore, can act as a sort of sociological 'BS' [abbreviation for bullshit, meaning rubbish, nonsense. *Oxford Dictionary of English*] detector. It provides a means of questioning the historical and cultural context of statements. It should alert us, for instance, when we hear statements to the effect that good manners are related to good breeding in its historical sense, or that slenderness is somehow more 'natural'. Likewise, when we hear statements such as, 'It's only natural for little girls to wear pink', we learn that it is nothing of the sort; it is a cultural convention for differentiating the sexes by the colour of their clothes or the paint in their room.

By way of illustrating further how these components of the sociological imagination operate together, consider the question of how we socially interact in everyday settings. A famous example of how history and culture combine is Erving Goffman's study on social interaction between individuals or small groups. Known as the dramaturgical model of social interaction, Goffman (1959) described how interaction between individuals followed a series of interaction rituals, which structured how everyday culture proceeded in countries like the United States. Goffman suggests that many interactions are like plays, including actors with roles and scripts, who put on performances. There is also a 'frontstage' and a 'backstage' where impression management and a release from the role for the actor occurs. There are two questions here about social interaction that we should consider using the socio-logical imagination. Firstly, why do we interact the way we do in public settings? Secondly, where do these forms of interaction come from? Both questions attempt to lift the lid on social inter-action by focusing on culture and history.

A common example of Goffman's backstage/frontstage version of social interaction, and one that many students who have casual or part time jobs in retail will relate to, is that of a rude customer. Let's say that a customer enters the store where you work and in the course of your interaction with them, they are rude, dismissive, and even abusive. They barely look at you, fiddle with their phone while you are trying to attend to their requests, talk over you, and so on. You, as an employee, are expected to keep smiling, attend to their needs, and be as polite as you can, despite whatever emotional upheavals you might otherwise be feeling. Because you are an employee, you are playing a certain role, you stick to a script, and perform due to necessity. This is the Goffmanian 'frontstage'. When you have finished your shift, how-ever, and are no longer playing the role, this is the 'backstage', and for a variety of reasons, you unload about your experience with the rude customer on a friend, social media, or to someone who will listen, all about how this rude customer made you enraged or miserable. What underlies this interaction and reaction, and what circumscribes Goffman's theory, is our cultural history associated with social roles of customer and retail assistance. Implicit in the roles of shop or retail assistant (in relation to customers) is not showing (negative) emotion, deference to different forms of social status and power (as an employee), and the development of eti-quette around social situations (a concern of Norbert Elias also, as we saw earlier in this chapter). This is learned, of course. Indeed many service type professions will provide training about how to deal with such customers as an important cultural approach to commerce, which is drawn from a history of social interaction around financial or commercial rituals.

Another example of how historical and cultural sensibilities operate together is the notion of sacred sites in modern society. Historically, because of their strong cultural and religious associations to the land, most First Nations cultures had and continue to have well-known sacred sites; that is, important spiritual places. Indeed, some of the major political struggles by First Nations peoples have been to preserve and protect these sites, such as the permanent ban on climbing Uluru (Ayers Rock) in Australia, at the request of the traditional owners, out of respect for its sacredness. What are the equivalents in secular industrialised societies? Religious buildings such as churches (especially cathedrals), mosques, and temples are obvious examples but other institutions also become imbued with spiritual meaning. Attempts to build shrines to capitalism, such as casinos and shopping malls, have failed to ignite much response and appear to do little to satisfy needs for spiritual observance. Instead what has become important are battle sites such as Gallipoli, where large amounts of the blood of young Australians and New Zealanders, as well of course of many Turks and those from other countries as well, was shed. Indeed an interesting sociological phenomenon has been the growth of 'pilgrimage'-like tourism, not only to the Dardenelles in Turkey but also the Kokoda trail in New Guinea and more recently the First World War battlefields of Flanders and France. In the United States, the Vietnam War Memorial in Washington increasingly has the character of a sacred site, something akin to those of First Nations peoples, as does the Gettysburg battlefield and Cu Chi in Vietnam (West 2017). Other candidates for secular sacred sites might be sporting arenas, such as the Melbourne Cricket Ground, Fenway Park in Boston, and Wembley Stadium in London. An historical and cultural sensitivity is important in developing an understanding of the meaning of these sites.

Conclusion

This chapter has considered the first two of the four components of a sociological imagination. Taking the two aspects of history and culture together is important, as Giddens (1983: 26) argues, because only with these two sensibilities in mind is it possible 'to break free from the straitjacket of thinking only in terms of the society we know in the here and now'. What we have today is the result, not of some preordained inevitable process of development but of a consequence of history and culture resulting in the unique organisation of the particular society in which we live. Being historically and culturally aware, avoiding being ahistorical or ethnocentric, are thus central components of a sociological imagination.

References

Armstrong, S., 1991. 'Female Circumcision: Fighting a Cruel Tradition', *New Scientist*, 2 February: 22–27.

Barker-Benfield, B., 1972. *Horrors of the Half-known Life*. Harper Torchbooks, New York.

Bauman, Z., 2000. *Liquid Modernity*. Wiley, London

Bellah, R., 1959. 'Durkheim and History', *American Sociological Review*, 24:4, 447–461.

Bourdieu, P., 1984 [1979]. *Distinction: a Social Critique of the Judgement of Taste*. Routledge & Kegan Paul, London.

Brisbane Courier Mail (newspaper). 2006. 'Toowoomba says no', 29 July [www.couriermail.com.au/news/special-features/toowoomba-says-no/news-story/54a3b4efdba73c8e7eb38f3c28cb0893].

Burns, A., Bottomley, G., and Jools, P. (eds), 1983, *The Family in the Modern World*. Allen & Unwin, Sydney.

Elias, N., 1978. *The Civilizing Process*. Urizen Books, New York.

Family Law Council, 1994. Female Genital Mutilation: Discussion Paper, 31 January, Canberra.

Giddens, A., 1983. *Sociology: a Brief but Critical Introduction*. Macmillan, London.

Giddens, A., 1991. *Modernity and Self-Identity: Self and Society in the Late Modern Age*. Stanford University Press, Stanford.

Goffman, E., 1959. *Presentation of Self in Everyday Life*. Anchor Books, New York.

Guardian (newspaper), 2013. 'Poll: are you happy to drink recycled sewage water?', 10 May [www.theguardian.com/environment/shortcuts/poll/2013/may/10/water-health].

Guardian (newspaper), 2017. 'Portugal's radical drugs policy is working. Why hasn't the world copied it?', 10 May [www.theguardian.com/environment/shortcuts/poll/2013/may/10/water-health].

Kipling, R., [1899] 2018. *Poems by Rudyard Kipling*. Franklin Classics, London.

Marx, K., 1988 [1932]. *The German Ideology*. Prometheus edition.

Mead, M., 1930. *Coming of Age in Samoa*. Morrow, New York.

Pew Research Centre, 2017. 'Muslims and Islam: key findings in the U.S. and around the world' [www.pewresearch.org/fact-tank/2017/08/09/muslims-and-islam-key-findings-in-the-u-s-and-around-the-world/].

Piketty, T., 2014. *Capital in the Twenty-First Century*. The Belknap Press of Harvard University Press, Cambridge Massachusetts.

Phillips, T., and Aarons, H., 2005. 'Choosing Buddhism in Australia: Towards a Traditional Style of Reflexive Engagement', *British Journal of Sociology*, 56:2, 215–232.

—— 2007 'Looking East: an Exploratory Analysis of Western Disenchantment', *International Sociology*, 22:3, 325–341.

Reeves, R., 2014. 'How to save marriage in America', *The Atlantic*, 14 February [www.theatlantic.com/business/archive/2014/02/how-to-save-marriage-in-america/283732/].

Roof, W., 2001. *Spiritual Marketplace: Babyboomers and the Remaking of the American Religion*. Princeton University Press, Princeton.

Shilling, C., 2003. *The Body and Social Theory*. Sage, London.

Smith, E., 2010. 'The Critical Reception of Shakespeare'. In De Grazia, M., and Wells, S. (eds), *The New Cambridge Companion to Shakespeare*. Cambridge University Press, Cambridge, 253–268.

Thomas, K., 1971. *Religion and the Decline of Magic: Studies in Popular Beliefs in Sixteenth and Seventeenth-Century England*. Penguin, London.

Turner, B., 1997, 'Understanding Change: Modernity and Postmodernity'. In Jureidini, R., Kenny, S., and Poole, M. (eds), *Sociology: Australian Connections*. Allen & Unwin, Sydney, 117–138.

Vera, H., 1989. 'On Dutch Windows', *Qualitative Sociology*, 12:2, 215–234.

Vogue, 2017. 'These Indonesian drag queens are shifting between genders and worlds', *Vogue*, 27 September [www.vogue.com/projects/13536497/drag-queens-indonesia-java-lgbtogue].

Weber, M., 2002. *The Protestant Ethic and the Spirit of Capitalism*. Penguin Books, Harmondsworth.

West, B. (ed.), 2017. *War, Memory, and Commemoration*. Routledge, New York

Wright Mills, C., 1959. *The Sociological Imagination*. Penguin, New York.

5 Structure and critique

This chapter considers the remaining two sensibilities of the sociological imagination. Whereas the historical and cultural components outlined in the previous chapter were elements to be taken into account in the analysis of social phenomena, the structural and critical components considered in this chapter indicate more styles of analysis, or ways of approaching the analysis.

Structural

Sociology is concerned with the relationship between the individual and society. This is a way of saying that, as a discipline, sociology is concerned with understanding the behaviour of individuals in the social context in which it occurs. To elucidate that social context, Sociologists often employ the notion of social structure as a conceptual tool or heuristic device (something which helps us with the analysis). These structures, it should be remembered, are not rigid and consensual – that is, everybody agrees this is what it should be like – but precarious and shifting. It is, after all is said and done, individuals that make structures and allow them to act as a source of constraint.

The quest for a sociological imagination involves developing a structural sensibility along with the various other types outlined. In trying to understand the social world, then, the social structure acts as a signpost to the sorts of questions to consider. As outlined earlier, the key sociological questions to ask are, 'What is it about the way our society is organised as a whole that would explain

DOI: 10.4324/9781003316329-5

this phenomenon?' and, 'How does the structure of society affect the behaviour of the individuals within it?' An example is that of shopping in the spiritual marketplace for religions such as Buddhism, as outlined earlier.

A structural sensibility leads us to consider whether all Westerners are involved in a spiritual quest that leads them to explore traditionally non-Western religions such as Buddhism, or some Westerners more than others? The trend in converting to or being involved with Buddhism is more pronounced amongst some class and occupational groups than others (Phillips and Aarons 2005; 2007). What is it about the way our society is organised that helps explain this phenomenon? In our view, it is a social structure related to the identity of being Western as well as occupation and education. In this context, the consequences of being Western, with its strong emphasis on material success, decline in trust and meaning in established religions such as Christianity, and the fracturing of community, produce a greater attraction to non-Western spiritualities in some sectors of society more than others. Those in the caring professions with higher levels of education (such as nursing or social work), in particular, being intimately associated with individuals in various states of trauma or distress, have made these Western spiritual seekers question the dominant or hegemonic cultural values of prioritising work, money, and material possessions. Turning to Buddhism – which for them, articulates more directly and meaningfully other life matters such as mental health, family, and ontological meaning – challenges the social structure and its impact on the individual.

A useful conceptual distinction that will assist in making sense of this element of the sociological imagination is the distinction between *agency* and *structure*. Do the actions of individual human beings (agents) create social structure, or does social structure constrain and create the actions of individuals? We can think of both agency and structure as being important but neither being solely responsible for a social phenomenon. Rather, it is a question of the relative combination of agency and structural factors.

Consider, for instance, that set of historic events we call the Second World War. Would it have happened at all if the particular human being, Adolf Hitler, had never been born? Explanations that stress the agency end of the continuum would say, 'No' – the events that followed were a direct result of (the agency of) that particular historical person. Explanations that stress the structure end of the continuum would be likely to respond, 'Probably, yes' – if Adolf Hitler had not come along to exploit the particular set of historical circumstances that existed in Weimar Germany in the 1920s, then some other particular person would have played the historical role that Hitler did. Similarly, the Second World War can be understood in structural terms (especially in the Pacific theatre) as being akin to a trade war, in which securing resources was important. Of course, adequate explanations of the Second World War require some elements of both structural and agency explanations.

Similarly, how are we to understand the remarkable historical events of rapid changes in the leadership of many countries? Australia, for example, had six changes of prime minister in the five years 2007–18, bringing unprecedented instability to the leadership position. To analyse one of these 'leadership spills' in more detail: in mid-2010 a first term prime minister, Kevin Rudd, was deposed by his party to be replaced by his deputy, who thereby became Australia's first female prime minister, Julia Gillard. What combination of agency issues (Julia Gillard's personality in particular) as against structural issues (a vitriolic campaign by the country's mining interests against a proposal to increase taxes paid), led to the downfall of Kevin Rudd?

Certainly the Press anyway have preferred explanations towards the agency end of the continuum. A more structural explanation would examine the then prime minister's lack of a factional base within the Australian Labor Party as well as policies that were the target of an aggressive campaign by a business sector only too well aware of the precedent-setting nature of this tax in their global operations of these large multinational mining countries that other sovereign countries may have been emboldened to follow (Bramston 2014). Similar analysis of the 2016 US presidential election should allow for agency factors such as the perceived populist appeal of Donald Trump, as well as the structural, in the form of the impact of decades of economic decline and perceived protracted neglect from mainstream

American presidential candidates in certain parts of the United States that helped produce Trump's victory.

A structural component of the sociological imagination is necessary to balance the ways in which history is sometimes taught in its 'great person' (or perhaps, more usually, 'great men') approach, as if agency was all that was at work and the course of history could be predominantly understood in terms of the personalities and motivations of political and other leaders. The argument being made in this book is for a position more on the structural side of the continuum; that the operation of those particular historical agents, important though their personalities were, can only be adequately understood within a broader structural context. It is not to argue that particular historical agents were unimportant, but for a greater emphasis on understanding the social context in which those events occurred. The debate is not just an academic one, it should be noted, but is relevant in understanding political events. Would slavery in the United States been abolished without Abraham Lincoln? Would the apartheid system in South Africa have ended if the particular historical person Nelson Mandela had never been born?

There is a lot of discussion these days about a style of politics called populism. Political populism, though not at all easily defined, can be thought of as a form of politics that promotes the 'pure people' against the 'corrupt elite' (Fieschi 2019). Populist political style has also been characterised by an 'us' and 'them' distinction that in some contexts promotes a strong emphasis on 'nationalist' and 'nativist' themes for a country's future betterment. An example of such nationalist statements is the familiar 'Make America Great Again' slogan made famous by Donald Trump. Populism is a style of politics that is practised by both the political far left (to some extent) but is mostly associated with the political far right, around issues of economic, cultural, and ethnic protection. Populist political parties and candidates have become familiar in everyday discourse on politics and are a feature of most national political landscapes. Donald Trump is perhaps the best-known populist candidate and the most successful to date, by becoming the president of the United States, but others such as Nigel Farage in the United Kingdom, and figures such as Clive

Palmer in Australia are also prominent. Trump and other individual politicians aside, the sociological question attempting to understand populism from a structural sensibility is 'What is it about the structure of society that produces this style of politics and politicians such as Donald Trump?'

The answer is complex but we can turn to a key contemporary structural change that has dramatically impacted Western societies, which will help explain the rise of populist politics around purity and protection.

This style of politics reflects an unease and insecurity on the part of many voters about the rapid pace of social change, which has been going on for decades, but more rapidly in recent years, gradually transforming the society people have known and in which they have lived. The political consequences have been that people have been less 'rusted on' to a conventional way of voting and there has been more volatility in electoral results. These changes, furthermore, have been felt in all Western democracies, aside from Australia, Great Britain, and the United States.

The processes of social change which are collectively known as *globalisation* are associated with late capitalism. Economies, and therefore societies, are being transformed as they become more internationally based. The transformation is from a blue-collar economy – that is, where a substantial proportion of the population earn their livelihood from working in manufacturing – to an economy in which many of these jobs are disappearing and other economic activity, such as service industries, come to dominate. For individuals, many of the old certainties about life are swept away in the course of economic reform. Jobs that were once performed on a secure, full-time basis have now been replaced in the name of labour market reform, with a large proportion of the population now earning their livelihoods from insecure, part-time, short-term jobs such as those characterised by what's known as the 'gig economy', which bear little relation to the traditional notion of a 'career'. For many workers, but perhaps especially for older men, the dignity of retiring at the end of a long and worthwhile career is being replaced by the ignominy of being squeezed out, laid off, and retrenched a decade or more earlier. Accompanying these profound economic changes are changes in demography and perceived threats to national culture and values due to mass migration, which in Europe has been a consequence of the tremendous turmoil in the Middle East. Further, as a result of such profound economic and social change, there is a loathing and distrust of a perceived global elite, whose incomes, way of life, and power are radically different from that of many ordinary citizens.

In such a situation, the 'politics of blame' focuses on migrants, on First Nations peoples, on welfare, and on crime through the 'us' and 'them' tropes mentioned earlier. Such economic change is leading to the polarisation of society between rich and poor, and between rural and urban. The anxiety expressed by the decline of the old order, in spite of indications that the economies emerging from a decade of recession and COVID-19 are reasonably robust and that part of their success has been due to immigration, has been powerfully reflected at the ballot box. Our point is that we do not get very far in our understanding of political events, such as elections and political style, by focusing (as the media tends to do) overwhelmingly on personalities. While these are not unimportant, what is also needed is a more structurally based account of what is occurring in the larger society, which will help explain the relative political instability associated with big changes in the political landscape. The ability of politicians to shape the society they are elected to govern is declining as powerful economic decisions are made by others with influence and international borders come to have less relevance.

A structural sensibility, therefore, is a necessary component of the sociological imagination. It means going beyond the level of individuals to take account of the broader structural context of the way in which that society is organised. Let's consider the ongoing HIV/AIDS epidemic as an example. One of the features of the epidemic has been that different countries are affected differently, some worse than others. African countries are among the worst affected. On every other continent, the number of people who have died or are infected with the HIV virus, which eventually leads to the onset of AIDS-related medical conditions and ultimately death, are measured in the thousands. In Africa, the number is measured in the millions. More than two thirds of all new HIV infections worldwide continue to be in sub-Saharan Africa, with women and girls at particular risk. In 2014, 91 per cent of the world's HIV-positive children lived in Africa. The number is now declining with antiretroviral treatment, although the extent of undiagnosed positives is unknown (UNAIDS 2021). Now, there is the added risk of COVID-19. By July 2021, less than 3 per cent of the population had received at least one dose of a COVID-19 vaccine (UNAIDS 2021).

Why has this epidemic been so bad on that continent? In trying to understand why the progression is much worse there than in other parts of the world, a structural component to the explanation is necessary. Explanations which focus only on individual components do not go far enough. It is also necessary to take into account issues to do with the social structure and organisation of many African societies. Why do young African women appear so prone to HIV infection?

In advanced economies, the AIDS pandemic, now entering its fourth decade in duration, has been primarily a homosexual phenomenon associated in particular with unprotected sex. In low-income societies, and in Africa in particular, the character of the pandemic is primarily heterosexual. It is both a sociological and a social problem with tragic consequences. In order to begin to answer this social and sociological problem, reference to the structure of these societies is necessary. In particular, some reference to the structure of power relationships between men and women in which men dominate, *patriarchy*, is an essential starting point. To a much greater extent than their Western sisters, African women find it difficult to negotiate about sexuality, as is characteristic of a highly patriarchal society. As a result, HIV prevalence is double that of men in many African countries (UNAIDS 2021). In one study 47 per cent of men and 40 per cent of women in Lesotho indicated that women have no right to refuse sex with their husbands or boyfriends (Andersson et al. 2007). In other words, social factors, such as relative powerlessness of women, are important.

There are other social factors as well. Economic opportunities for people to gain livelihoods are structured in such a way that migration in search of work is a major feature of the pattern of life. Many people, particularly African men, must spend long periods away from their homes due to work activities. In such a context the usual constraints on multiple sexual partners are lessened and the likelihood of HIV transmission is much greater. In other words, the spread of the virus has less to do with the characteristics of individuals and more to do with the organisation of the society in which they live.

Failure to take adequate account of the structural level leads to a common way of thinking in our society, which the quest for sociological understanding attempts to overcome. Focusing only on the individual level of analysis to the exclusion of the structural level encourages a sort of rationale or justification for the social phenomena called the *ideology of victim blaming*. Victim blaming occurs when individuals themselves are held to be responsible for what happens to them. It fails to engage a structural sensibility to also help explain what occurs.

An example is rape. While there has arguably been some change for the better in recent times, there is still often the assumption that the woman somehow deserved what happened to her. Either she was wearing clothes that from a male point of view could be defined as 'provocative', she was walking in a 'dangerous' place at an inappropriate time (late at night), she was assumed to have encouraged the man in such a way he was justified to interpret it as a 'come-on', or said, 'No' when he assumed she really meant 'Yes'. In other words, the victim is blamed for what occurred. This approach, still often seized upon by defence counsel as an appropriate line when defending charges of rape, pays inadequate attention to the structural context of patriarchal gender relations in this and other societies, or indeed the rights of women to wear what they want, go where they want or generally act as they want. In all, the victims are blamed for acting like autonomous, 'free' members of a society of which they comprise more than 50 per cent! Having a structural sensibility is therefore important to avoiding this sort of 'blaming the victim' response, which the lack of a sociological understanding often engenders.

Another example of blaming the victim was discussed previously in the example of health and safety at work. Explanations for what have traditionally been called 'industrial accidents' have usually been couched in terms of 'accident-proneness'. As was argued earlier, this explanation for what should be more appropriately called 'occupational injury' fails to take account of the structural context in which employer–employee relationships are constructed. One structural constraint of this relationship is the requirement that expensive machinery be operated on a 24-hour basis, making shift work necessary. Working at night under conditions akin to permanent jet lag predisposes workers to more injuries, proportionately speaking, than on day shifts. This .is hardly surprising to anyone who has ever worked night shift when their body's circadian rhythms become out of kilter and they have difficulty getting adequate sleep in urban environments during the daytime. To blame workers for the injuries that occur is by no means the whole story and does not take adequate notice of the production relations under which employment occurs.

This is not to argue that the individual level of analysis has no bearing on understanding the phenomenon. Rather, it is to argue that we do not get very far in our analysis of society if we focus only on the individual level. This issue is tied up with the extent to which individuals are responsible for their own actions. Individual workers may be careless, or indeed stupid, resulting in injury to themselves or others at work. But that is not the whole story. The design of jobs for maximum productivity rather than any sense of job satisfaction or personal enrichment may lead to careless or silly behaviour out of extreme boredom. Furthermore, failing to observe safety procedures may not just be a matter of worker irresponsibility, but a quite reasonable response to a particular set of circumstances.

The wearing of ear muffs (also more formally known as hearing protection) to minimise hearing loss when working in noisy environments is an example of the last point above. Quite apart from the fact that they represent fitting the worker to the job rather than vice versa (installing quieter machinery which would remove the need for ear muffs), their effectiveness is limited if one also wears spectacles; they are uncomfortable to wear in hot, humid environments; and they virtually prevent any communication between fellow workers (about the only thing that can lessen the boredom).

A feature of the structural component of a sociological imagination, therefore, is that we should be suspicious of explanations for social phenomena based on some notion of irrationality on the part of the people involved. Indeed, in the quest for sociological understanding of the social world, it is another component of our sociological 'bullshit' detector. What may appear irrational at the level of the individual, may appear quite different when the wider social structural context is taken into account. Definitions of rationality, in fact, are often culturally bound.

A structural sensibility is important in understanding many aspects of society. One thing that bothers people today, for example, is the apparent decline in the quality of customer service in retailing. Shopping is a major form of leisure activity – aptly summed up by the phrase, 'shop till you drop' (see Prus and Dawson 1991). Retail spending online during the COVID-19 pandemic lockdowns soared to new heights (*Sydney Morning Herald* 2021). Yet the enjoyment of this form of leisure is often diminished by what are considered to be the attitude problems of retailing staff in a reversal of the Goffmanian example offered earlier: surly, indifferent, and sullen, with not enough of them, especially in the large department and chain retailing stores. What was assumed to be some golden age of retailing service in the past has been replaced by self-service and the rise and rise of online shopping. A structural sensibility would indicate that to blame the employees alone for the decline in customer service is not the whole story, as many of the readers of this book who earn a part-time living in retailing will know only too well. Indeed it has an element of 'blaming the victim' about it. The more structural explanation would focus on how, in an effort to improve their competitive position, retailers have moved to mass discount pricing.

In order to stay profitable with reduced margins, employers have sought to cut costs – especially labour costs. In other words, employers have sought to improve their competitive position at the expense of their workers. The result has not only been less full-time retailing jobs but also the creation of retailing jobs that involve part-time employment, increased workloads, few prospects for advancement, little job security, and declining pay.

Most jobs have been made more routine, involving lower-skilled tasks such as cash register operation and shelf stocking. Lower staff training costs is the aim. In this situation the 'attitude' problems of retailing staff are perhaps more understandable. It is little wonder that service has declined.

A structural sensibility is also often crucial when attempting to understand major social problems. One of the foremost of these in the Australian context is the continued existence of a population enclave of the original First Nations population, whose health and other living standards are akin to those of some of the poorest countries – in a country that otherwise prides itself on being one of the most developed in the world. For many white Australians, the most visible sign of this is drunkenness amongst the First Nations population. Viewing such drunken behaviour is wont to bring out the latent racism that many white Australians harbour. Victim blaming appears quickly as an explanation for the behaviour observed. Yet a structural sensibility tells another story entirely.

Alcohol abuse is a major social problem in some First Nations communities. Many have banned or are attempting to ban its sale within community boundaries. The 2007 Intervention by the Howard Federal Government was another broader attempt in this direction. Data collected on a national scale shows the extent of the problem in recent history. While the proportion of First Nations Australians who don't drink alcohol at all is increasing, of those who do consume alcohol, a greater proportion does so at levels that pose both short-term and long-term risks to their health and the health of others (Gray et al. 2018). In the period 2014–18, First Nations males died from alcohol-related causes at 4.3 times the rate of non-First Nations males, and First Nations females at 4.7 times the rate of non-First Nations females (AIHW 2018).

Although there have been improvements in 'closing the gap' between First Nations and non-First Nations populations in recent decades, the damage to health is part of a health pattern seen most often in a developing country, not a developed one. In 2015–17, after adjusting for age structure between the two populations, life expectancy for First Nations Australians is 71 years for males and 75 for females. The gap between First Nations and non-First Nations Australians life expectancy was 8.6 years for males and 7.8 years for females. The rate of infant and child mortality is twice the rate for white Australians (AIHW 2018). Tuberculosis, trachoma, and leprosy, all found in First Nations communities, are practically unknown amongst white Australians (SJC 1991: 209–210). Poor health status is both a feature and a result of a general malaise within First Nations communities and it is also reflected in unemployment rates, which are many times higher than those found in white communities. Subsequent attempts to extinguish native title to land, and the poor state of First Nations health, should be obvious. Extinguishment in 1998 of the last vestiges of native title under the Wik decision in the name of giving 'certainty' to pastoralists has only worsened First Nations health problems, including those involving alcohol.

The contrast with the New Zealand situation is instructive. While considered only a beginning and in no way a panacea for ameliorating racial problems, the gradual legal recognition through the 1980s of the Treaty of Waitangi, first signed in 1840, has had symbolic and legal consequences in recognising the importance of land ownership to cultural identity (see Orange 1989). It has also provided a basis upon which issues of disputed land ownership can be resolved through a special tribunal established for this express purpose. But even when governments have attempted to recognise the link between land and cultural identity, however symbolic, widespread racist attitudes on the part of the white population have sometimes stymied the attempts. Changing place names back to their original First Nations names is one such example.

A decision taken in Victoria in 1991 to restore the name of the Grampians National Park in central Victoria to the original First Nations name of Gariwerd met with a hostile response from some local white Australians, who threatened to tear down the signs announcing the name changes. An early decision by an incoming conservative state government in 1993 reversed the decision, ironically coinciding with the beginning of the International Year of Indigenous Peoples. In the New Zealand context, similar name changes have occurred with widespread local white opposition – for instance, when the decision was made to call that most beautiful of New Zealand mountains by its original Maori name, first as Mt Taranaki and then as *Taranaki Maunga*, instead of Mt Egmont, the name given to it by Captain James Cook after an English aristocrat. In the recent settlements of tribal land claims, one in the South Island will see the name of Aotearoa's highest mountain revert officially to *Aorangi* ('cloud piercer') instead of Mt Cook. Now there is a political movement growing in favour of replacing the name of the whole nation New Zealand with the Maori original '*Aotearoa*'.

To recap, the argument being made is that an adequate understanding of the problem of alcohol abuse in some First Nations communities can only begin by considering the structural context of First Nations people in a predominantly white Australian society. This does not make it less of a problem, it should be said, nor does it absolve First Nations alcohol abusers from responsibility for the damage caused. What it does say, though, is that we will not get very far in our understanding of the problem, which is an essential precursor to trying to ameliorate the problem, if we remain only at the level of the individuals themselves. Our sociological BS detector should tell us that blaming or 'cracking down' on the abusers is not likely to get us very far.

A structural sensibility, along with the other components of a sociological imagination, is crucial in the quest for sociological understanding of the social world. It is an aspect of the sociological imagination that is sometimes misunderstood. These structures are not necessarily fixed, rigid, and settled. Instead they may be fluid, constantly evolving and contested. As outlined, when attempting to understand some aspects of the society in which we live, it is a way of orienting to a broader group level of analysis; of asking, 'What is it about the way our society is organised that results in this or that occurring?' It is, as Berger (1963) argues, understanding the particular in terms of the general; how what happens to individuals can be 'made sense of' sociologically speaking in terms of what's happening in society as a whole. When it happens to one person it is idiosyncratic and anecdotal. When it happens to lots of people in one society, such as to constitute a pattern or a regularity, then that's when

Sociologists get interested (indeed fascinated, some even excited!), especially if it gives some insight into what is happening to our society as a whole.

Critical

The final component of a sociological imagination is the critical component. Here, it is important to note, the term 'critical' is being used somewhat differently from its common meaning of being negative about something. Rather, the term is used in Sociology as being reflexive or sceptical about the social world, and of being engaged in a *critique* of the existing social world. A critical sensibility is implied, as outlined in Chapter 2, by the last two questions to be asked in trying to understand a particular social phenomenon from a sociological point of view: '*How do you know?*' and '*How could it be otherwise?*'

Applying a critical sensibility means engaging in *systematic* doubt about accounts of the social world. Not all accounts of the social world are likely to be equally accurate, so the basis on which the quest for sociological understanding can proceed is that of scepticism about the claim of any statement to be a valid account of a particular matter. It is a way of proceeding which aims to narrow the range of doubt as much as possible. In exercising a critical sensibility, competing explanations for particular social phenomena are approached by trying to uncover and expose as many as possible of the ambiguities, misrepresentations, distortions, and even falsehoods among those competing claims. It seeks to *demystify* these competing explanations by exposing them to systematic doubt.

A critical sensibility has two components. The first is common to all intellectual and scientific endeavour and concerns the use of evidence. Asking, '*How do you know?*' is a way of considering both, 'What's your evidence?' and, 'Is the claim you are making justified in the light of what we already know about the social world, or are you going beyond that?' Being critical does not mean only being negative: it may eventually mean being positive about something. What it does mean is carefully considering the evidence that is available before deciding your position.

There is also a second level, more specific to the quest for sociological understanding of the social world, that of asking, '*How could it be otherwise?*' Opposing the view that Sociology can and should emulate the natural and physical sciences in its method of understanding the world, Giddens (1983: 26) states:

> No social processes are governed by unalterable laws. As human beings we are not condemned to be swept along by forces that have the inevitability of laws of nature. But this means we must be conscious of the *alternative futures* that are potentially open to us. [Here] the sociological imagination fuses with the task of Sociology in contributing to *the critique of existing forms of society*.
>
> (Emphasis in original)

As we have seen, sociology emerged in the nineteenth century as an attempt to understand the massive social changes brought about by the French and Industrial Revolutions. This traditional focus remains central. As Tepperman (1994: vii) argues: 'Even today, Sociology remains, at its core, a debate about the human ability to improve social life through reason and organised action'.

The sociological quest involves not only description and explanation to demonstrate what is, it also involves asking *what might be*. No particular vision of what might be is dictated by this application of the sociological imagination. Indeed, different Sociologists will frequently have different recommendations of what should be done in a particular situation. It is the concern with critique itself that is a crucial aspect of the quest for sociological understanding. As Giddens (1983: 166) argues, 'As critical theory, Sociology does not take the social world as given but poses the questions: what types of social change are feasible and desirable and how should we strive to achieve them?' This, he adds, is because Sociology, along with the social sciences in general, 'is inherently and inescapably part of the subject matter it seeks to comprehend'.

The question of what alternative futures are possible and desirable inevitably raises questions of values and objectivity, which are present in all academic disciplines. Can the quest for sociological understanding be value-free? Can personal values and experiences be put aside when social phenomena are approached for study? Can *bias* (interpreting evidence according to one's values) be avoided? These questions have been the subject of considerable debate in the discipline.

It is now widely accepted that the sorts of values held by people in general, and therefore by social scientists such as Sociologists as well, are bound to influence all that they think and feel and how they act. What topics are chosen for investigation, how those sociological problems are investigated, and what sort of conclusions are reached will all be influenced by personal values. The common position taken in the discipline today, following Gouldner (1973), is that the same critically reflexive approach to the study of social phenomena in general should also be applied to the question of values. In this book, for instance, the examples chosen to illustrate the argument reflect, to a certain extent, our interests and therefore our values.

Arguing this position on values is not to say that objectivity is not important. Rather, it is a recognition that it is necessary to work out when these values should be kept out of the teaching or research process (such as in the interpretation of research findings) and when they should be expressed, not attempting to be value-free. For instance, we have implied in this book that female genital mutilation is outrageous and has no place in modern society. We have also said that immigration has contributed to the recent economic success of the advanced economies. These are examples of our values and many readers may not agree with them. Expressing them here is not dictating to readers but challenging them to make up their own minds about the issues at hand.

The point is that saying what sorts of social change are desirable and feasible is very much a part of the sociological imagination. We might not agree, for instance, on the extent to which land rights will ameliorate the conditions of the original inhabitants of countries such as Australia and New Zealand, but discussing and arguing the issue is as much a part of the quest for sociological understanding as is the task of describing and explaining the situation. Indeed Coulson and Riddell (1970: 86) go further and state, 'The claim that non-controversial value-free Sociology can develop in a conflict based social structure is theoretically untenable, practically unrealistic and morally and politically disastrous'.

Critique is an important part of what Sociologists do. It is this debunking or demystifying aspect of the sociological imagination that has given the discipline its somewhat controversial character. It arises from the tendency of Sociologists, as part of the quest for sociological understanding, to challenge official explanations for things or to challenge those in authority who have a particular vested interest in reality being portrayed in a particular way, much like the way populist politicians do. For example, it is both convenient and comfortable for rich people to believe they are overtaxed and that poverty no longer exists, or it is the fault of the individual, so the amount of tax they pay appears excessive. High income earners, on the basis of published statistics, actually pay a lower proportion of their income in tax than the rest of the population, and that the proportion of the total wealth of the country owned by the top few per cent of the population is increasing. The 30-year trend of rising inequality has continued with the richest boosting their share of income significantly over recent years in spite of the Global Financial Crisis (GFC). According to the 'Credit Suisse global wealth report' (2018) the world's richest 1 per cent, those with more than $1 million, own 43.4 per cent of the world's wealth. Indeed the richest 10 men in the world have as much wealth as many whole countries (Inequality.org 2018). Their data also shows that adults with less than $10,000 in wealth make up 53.6 per cent of the world's population but hold just 1.4 per cent of global wealth. The top 1 per cent of taxpayers are the richest they've been, in relative terms, since the 1950s, even after the ravages of the GFC (*Sydney Morning Herald* 2015) and the COVID-19 pandemic (Inequality. org 2018).

What Sociologists say about any issue may cut across moral, political, or religious beliefs. Indeed, Sociology is sometimes accused of being inherently subversive. This is certainly not the case in the sense of promoting radical social change of a revolutionary nature, and generations of students who have come to the discipline expecting this have been sorely disappointed. Rather, the sensitivity to critique is to ask questions about what else is possible and not assume that the current social organisation of society is somehow ordained or the only one. It is, of course, not only Sociology that experiences this controversial character. Any person or organisation seeking to understand how our society actually operates may experience it, even an official government body.

The debunking and demystification that is so much a part of the sociological imagination is concerned with challenging the myths or ideologies by which society operates. An example is the so-called 'rule of law'. It is an important part of the socialisation of children in society that they are taught the law is just, wise, good, and to be obeyed. Sociologists, however, have asked, 'Who makes the law?' 'Whose interests are being protected?' and, 'Who benefits the most from laws being organised the way they are?' Several decades of intensive research have led to the conclusion that it is the rich and powerful who benefit from the rule of law – especially as the cost of legal representation outstrips the ability of all but the most wealthy to afford it – and that most of the operation of the rule of law is directed at keeping the poor and the powerless in line. Critiquing the rule of law is not the same as advocating its overthrow, however (recent defunding of the police protests in the United States notwithstanding). Rather, it is to ask questions such as, 'How could the law work better?'

So the quest for sociological understanding involves the sensitivity to critique. To ask the most relevant questions sociologically will include asking, 'Who benefits?' (all of society, or some much more than others?) Does the 'golden rule' apply here? Do those that have the gold tend to rule? This is the controversial character of the discipline. It is why departments of Sociology have not traditionally been found at the main establishment institutions of higher learning such as Oxford and Cambridge, or in the Australian universities such as Sydney, Melbourne, or Adelaide, which model themselves on the English institutions. Sociology as a discipline is taught at all these places but, unlike most other institutions throughout the world, not in separate departments of Sociology but in the context of politics, education, or anthropology courses.

Structural and critical considerations together

Finally, some examples will illustrate how the structural and critical components of the sociological imagination operate together to provide an understanding of certain aspects of our society, especially as they relate to policies developed to deal with them. One example is the situation of endangered animal species. We face the prospect of a number of the world's animal species being hunted to extinction, or at least lost from their natural surroundings entirely, existing only in zoos. Pandas, rhinoceroses, and tigers are just a few on the edge of extinction. The number of tigers, for instance, is estimated to have declined by 95 per cent during the twentieth century, to no more than 5000–7500 (WWF 2000). Longer-term threats loom for many other animals, including gorillas, elephants, and wolves. The dominance of homo sapiens (us) in the animal kingdom is making it difficult for others to survive. Two different processes are threatening the survival of species. The more general one is the result of the exponential growth in our world population. The clearing of rainforest, the subsistence hunting of other animals in the food chain on whom these large animals prey, such as deer, pigs, and wild cattle, all make survival precarious for many species.

The other more specific threat is poaching for illegal trade in body parts. There is a cultural component to this. The products, such as rhinoceros' horn or tiger parts, are valuable in Asian countries because of their supposed medicinal value. Tiger penis soup, for instance, is prescribed to restore flagging libidos! Yet even here a structural understanding is important. In a situation reminiscent of opium growers participating in the drug trade in poorer countries, so poachers faced with poverty and the need to feed families perhaps understandably see poaching as a source of economic survival. Critical thinking also helps understanding with a parallel example: the destruction of endangered species for their short-term use makes about as much sense as burning a famous bark painting to provide heating!

Another example is the official policy towards the unemployed. Some aspects to this policy are the assumptions that the cause of unemployment is lack of job skills on the part of the individual and that the threat of removing unemployment benefits after a period of time will maintain unemployed people's motivation to keep searching for jobs. Hence the requirement that training courses of some sort or another must be undertaken in order to qualify for continued benefits. Both aspects, however, are based on the assumption that the cause of unemployment exists at the individual level of the beneficiaries themselves – that the factors stopping them getting a job are to do with them personally rather than with the structural situation of the economy as a whole. Yet when the ratio of job seekers to advertised jobs has been as high as 30 to 1, the ability of individual job seekers to find employment is bound to be enormously frustrating. The requirement to take courses to retain benefits is in some ways akin to polishing up the unemployed only to put them back on the shelf at the end of the process.

This is not to say that training courses are not relevant. At the level of maintenance or development of self-esteem they may be important. But considering the structural level of analysis, solving the now major problem facing our societies – that there is not enough work for those who require it – will not be achieved by focusing on the individual and in effect blaming them for the situation in which they find themselves. Analysing the situation critically reveals a paradox: that attempts by government to wind back spending on welfare by restricting outlays in various areas have consequences in other areas. A significant proportion of the fit, active population is idle at the very time when reductions in government spending are depriving the state of the basic infrastructure of the society. Public facilities, such as schools, are poorly maintained. Walking tracks in national parks are falling into disrepair through lack of maintenance. Services providing help for the disabled are under great strain due to lack of funding. What alternative futures are possible to overcome this paradox? Some system of matching the needs in one area to the availability of solutions in another is clearly necessary.

The final example of how the structural and critical sensitivities operate together is the phenomenon of mass killings, which have shocked many in recent times. The examples are becoming legion: Hoddle Street and Queen Street in Melbourne, Strathfield in Sydney, Columbine High School in Colorado, Paradise Nevada, Port Arthur in Tasmania, Montreal in Quebec, and Christchurch in New Zealand, to mention just a few. Multiple victim shootings by a lone gunman have caused great anguish in societies

The individual level of understanding is obviously very important to analysing these events. The individuals concerned and their states of psychological health are very relevant. But the individual level of analysis is not enough; an understanding of the structural level is also needed. Here it is necessary to consider such aspects as a culture of masculinity in which both violence towards others is an acceptable solution to personal difficulties (reflected in such phenomena as domestic violence), and guns are akin to an expression of masculinity itself. Attempts to restrict the availability of weapons, in particular automatic guns for which there can be no reasonable justification for allowing public own- ership in peacetime, have met with staunch opposition from vocal lobby groups. Observe groups of small boys (rarely girls) playing together. Playing with toy guns and simulating shootings are very much a part of the socialisation into masculine culture that young boys undergo. Parents who refuse to allow their chil- dren to have toy guns find their sons turning any stick or Lego® construction into a weapon shape. Then there are other struc- tural considerations, including how we are desensitised to vio- lence by the continual exposure to mainly American television and movie scripts in which gratuitous violence, filled with gun- toting cult figures, is part of virtually every plot. Video games also glorify violence – one such game was advertised, complete with marketing language, 'You'll soon be up to your waist in blood and guts'! Recent movies such as the Korean contribution 'Squid Game' in the survival thriller genre are almost gleefully vicious and violent.

We also need to consider the situation in which these unfor- tunate individuals find themselves. As all the inquests into the various shootings have found, there are many individuals like these gunmen in the community. In the context of the running down of public mental health services, deinstitutionalisation of the men- tally ill and the possible isolation of individuals even in small com- munities, it is virtually certain such calamities will occur again.

Again, it is worth explaining since this is an aspect of the sociological imagination that is sometimes misunderstood, which is not to say that the individuals concerned are not responsible for their actions and should not face the consequences. What we are saying is that focusing on the individual alone leaves an explanation incomplete. In a sense, the perpetrators are victims themselves. Furthermore, we will not get very far in our attempts to understand social phenomena like these slayings, to be able to prevent them occurring in the future, unless we consider the wider context in which they take place. Likewise with the availability of guns. While they greatly exacerbate the dangers of violence, from a structural perspective, no one suggests that restricting gun usage to law enforcement officers would somehow 'solve' the social problems faced in our society. Although guns make the violence much worse, the underlying causes of violence are not guns per se, but other more social factors, including poverty and racism.

Conclusion

This chapter has considered the structural and critical aspects of the sociological imagination. We have argued here and in the previous chapter that the quest for a sociological understanding of a particular phenomenon involves exercising the four sensibilities, which are historical, cultural, structural, and critical. Engaging in sociological analysis of some aspect of the social world requires a consideration of each of these aspects in turn. Each is partial, but together they represent the hallmark of a sociological way of understanding the social world.

References

AIHW (Australian Institute of Health and Welfare), 2018. '2.16 Risky alcohol consumption' [www.indigenoushpf.gov.au/].

Andersson, N., Ho-Foster, A., Mitchell, S., Scheepers, E., and Goldstein, S., 2007. 'Risk Factors, for Domestic Physical Violence: National Cross-Sectional Household Surveys in Eight Southern African Countries', *BMC Women's Health*, 7:11 [www.biomedcentral.com/1472-6874/7/11].

Berger, P., 1963. *An Invitation to Sociology.* Penguin, New York.

Bramston, T., 2014. 'Rudd, Gillard and beyond', Penguin e-Books [www.penguin.com.au/books/rudd-gillard-and-beyond-penguin-special-9781743485163].

Coulson, M., and Riddell, D., 1970. *Approaching Sociology: a Critical Introduction.* Routledge, London.

Credit Suisse (Bank), 2020. 'Credit Suisse global wealth report', Credit Suisse Research Institute [www.credit-suisse.com/about-us-news/en/articles/media-releases/global-wealth-report-2020-202010.html].

Fieschi, C., 2019. *Populocracy: The Tyranny of Authenticity and the Rise of Populism.* Agenda Publishing, Newcastle upon Tyne.

Giddens, A., 1983. *Sociology: a Brief but Critical Introduction.* Macmillan, London.

Gouldner, A., 1973, 'Anti-Minotaur: the Myth of a Value-Free Sociology'. In Gouldner, A., *For Sociology: Renewal and Critique in Sociology Today.* Allen Lane, London.

Gray D., Cartwright, K., Stearne, A., Saggers, S., Wilkes, E., and Wilson, M., 2018. 'Review of the harmful use of alcohol among Aboriginal and Torres Strait Islander people', Australian Indigenous HealthInfoNet [https://healthinfonet.ecu.edu.au/key-resources/resources/35480/?title=Review+of+the+harmful+use+of+alcohol+among+Aboriginal+and+Torres+Strait+Islander+people+%5Bvideo%5D&contentid=35480_1].

Inequality.org, 2018. 'Global inequality', Institute for Policy Studies [https://inequality.org/facts/global-inequality/].

Orange, C., 1989. *The Story of a Treaty.* Allen & Unwin, Wellington.

Phillips, T., and Aarons, H., 2005. 'Choosing Buddhism in Australia: Towards a Traditional Style of Reflexive Engagement', *British Journal of Sociology*, 56:2, 215–232.

—— 2007. 'Looking East: an Exploratory Analysis of Western Disenchantment', *International Sociology*, 22:3, 325–341.

Prus, R., and Dawson, L., 1991. 'Shop Till You Drop: Shopping as Recreational and Laborious Behaviour', *Canadian Journal of Sociology*, 16:2, 145–164.

SJC (Social Justice Collective), 1991. *Inequality in Australia.* Heinemann, Melbourne.

Sydney Morning Herald (newspaper), 2015. Richest 1 per cent own half the world's wealth: report (smh.com.au).

—— 2021. 'COVID Australia: Bricks and mortar retail stores post-lockdown comeback', 21 December [www.smh.com.au/business/the-economy/we-still-love-to-browse-bricks-and-mortar-stores-make-post-lockdown-comeback-20211220-p59j1w.html].

Tepperman, L., 1994. *Choices and Chances: Sociology for Everyday Life*, 2nd edn. Harcourt Brace, Toronto.

UNAIDS, 2021. '2021 Global AIDS update' [www.unaids.org/en/resources/presscentre/pressreleaseandstatementarchive/2021/july/20210714_global-aids-update].

WWF (World Wildlife Fund), 2000. 'Population estimates of existing wild tigers in 2000'. [www.worldwildlife.org/tigers/population.cfm].

6 The social and the biological world

Having outlined the four sensibilities involved in developing an adequate sociological analysis, we propose now to illustrate one important way in which they can be used: to analyse and discuss the boundary between the natural and the social worlds. The debate about the relative importance of environment and hereditary factors, about nature and nurture, is a long one and has all sorts of political implications. To what extent is biology social destiny? To what extent is the way a person turns out as he or she grows from childhood to adulthood the result of the particular genetic configuration they received at birth, and to what extent is it the result of the social experiences they have while growing up? The answers are complex and difficult to do justice to in a book of this size and introductory character. But they clearly involve some combination of both factors; the debate is where the relative emphasis should be put.

The social and biological worlds

The nature–nurture debate has intensified in recent years with the advent of the Human Genome Project, the huge scientific project based in the United States in which molecular biologists and geneticists mapped the human genetic structure. The potential for genetic engineering is that much closer. Certain diseases which have historically caused enormous suffering may eventually be eliminated. But some aspects of the programme are controversial, especially in the area of behavioural genetics. Critics of

DOI: 10.4324/9781003316329-6

the project, however, say it puts too much emphasis on genetic causes of behaviour and too little on environmental and social causes (see Hubbard and Wald 1993).

How does a sociological imagination inform these debates? How do Sociologists differentiate between the social and the biological world? Sociologists, while accepting the importance of genetic/hereditary factors have generally tended to stress more the environment/nurture side of the continuum. In other words, they would generally stress the importance of the social in drawing the boundary between the social and the biological world.

The need to differentiate the effects of the natural as against the social world is well established amongst Sociologists. This is reflected in the conceptual terminology used, and a couple of important conceptual distinctions can be made. The first concerns how the period in the life course of an individual from the age of about 12 to 25 years should be conceptualised. Should it be seen as the period of *adolescence* or of *youth*? 'Adolescence' is the term most often used in medical and other circles to refer to a particular stage of physical and psychological development in the human life cycle culminating in 'maturity'. In sociological terms, however, this concept is not very useful for analysing the complex social and cultural factors affecting young people's lives, when they are no longer children but are not yet accepted as adults. (The concept of adolescence is of relatively recent historical origin and refers to young people in industrialised countries.)

Historically, the transition between childhood and adulthood for all but the children of the affluent was much shorter and harsher. However, in industrialised countries at least, the abolition of child labour, the extension of the period of full-time education and the continuing economic dependence on parents, often well into a person's third decade of life, has created a time characterised by ambiguity, which is most usefully described as 'youth'. In today's times of casualised and generally poor job opportunities, as well as declining housing affordability, it is perhaps much harder for a greater proportion of young people to move out of home and establish their own independent livelihood and living arrangements than it was for their parents a generation ago. 'Adult children' in their twenties and thirties living at home with their parents are a common occurrence today, a situation exacerbated by the COVID-19 pandemic when many had little option but to move back home after losing their jobs. The key features of this period in a person's life cannot be tightly defined as a biophysiological category. When it begins and ends has enormous variation. Indeed there is nothing biologically determined about the experience of young people; their experience is the outcome of changing historical, cultural, and structural circumstances. Does the twenty-first birthday party today retain the element of marking the status passage from child to adult as it may have done in the past? Does anyone actually get their first key to the family home at twenty-one?

Another essential distinction is between *sex* and *gender*. Sex refers to the biological differences between men and women, especially in genitalia. Gender refers to the meaning attached to being male or female, both historically and culturally. Little girls traditionally wear pink clothing while little boys wear blue. These are the colours we have come to associate with being male or female. At this time, both historically and culturally, these are the social meanings that have become attached to the fact of being male or female. Over time these meanings have become much more fluid and contested with the rise of the LBGTQI+ community and even intersex public restrooms. As with ethnicity, it is important to note that everyone has a gender; it is not something that only women have, which is how it is sometimes used!

The distinction between sex and gender is necessary because the biological does not determine the social; biology is of minimal importance with regard to the place of women (or men) in any society. The range of meaning attached to being female or male in any society varies enormously, culturally and historically. The social construction of the meaning of being male or female is usually discussed in terms of the concepts of *masculinity* and *femininity*. Sociologists have found it useful to talk about masculinity and femininity as social practices; that is, as being grounded in practical actions in terms of what people do. In this way they are able to talk about gendered practices, such as wearing pink or blue, as social not biological.

An example of gender difference is the attitude towards body hair. For many Western women in this historical period, body hair in armpits, on legs, and on 'bikini lines' is something to be removed, often with considerable discomfort. This is not something that men in our society usually worry about, except on their faces. One sometimes hears the argument that it is more 'natural' for women to remove body hair. Our 'BS' detector should switch to 'red alert' here. It is, of course, nothing of the sort, but a part of the traditional social practice of femininity, acknowledging that there are *social mores* (behavioural expectations) in this historical and cultural context for women to shave their legs. Once again, a wander through an art gallery will show you how recent this concern this. Luxurious tufts of armpit hair on the female as well as the male figures were once common. Our sociological imagination should make us extremely sceptical whenever claims about something being more natural are made.

The development of a particular sociological language or jargon can also be seen as an attempt to be precise about issues such as the boundary between the social and the biological world. A couple of examples will make this clearer.

The first example to be explored concerns the ratio of women to men and what has been called the 'missing 100 million women' (Sen 1990). On the terrain of sex – that is, from the science of human reproductive biology – we know that about 5 per cent more boys than girls are born. But women are biologically hardier than men and, if both sexes receive the same care, women survive better than men at all ages (Ritchie and Roser 2019). So the sex ratio that would be expected is about 105 women to every 100 men. But the gender ratio, which is a different measure reflecting the outcome of social conditions, can be different.

In most Western countries, such as the United States, Canada, Australia, New Zealand, Great Britain, and France, the sex ratio and the gender ratio coincide. Women outnumber men. The ratio is roughly 105 women for every 100 men. In many countries of Asia and North Africa, however, the pattern is very different. The sex ratio (that is, from reproductive biology) continues at 105:100 but the gender ratio does not. In Egypt the ratio is 95 females for every 100 males, in Bangladesh, China, and West Africa, 94:100; in India, 93:100; and in Pakistan, 90:100. The difference between the sex ratio that should be expected and the gender ratio of what actually occurs is estimated by the United Nations to amount to, in Sen's estimate, 77 million women. He later revised this figure to 100 million and more recent research has suggested a deficit of as many as 126 million, mainly in China and India (Bongaarts and Guilmoto 2015). There are vastly fewer women than reproductive biology would lead us to expect. Why?

The quest for a sociological explanation for these startling figures begins by asking, 'What is it about the way those societies are organised that might explain the difference?' The answer needs historical, cultural, structural, and critical sensibilities. If the proportion of women to men is substantially less than would be expected and less than other countries in the world, there must be aspects of the way those societies are organised that will account for the difference. Sen (1992) points to a range of practices that help explain these figures, all resulting from the organisation of the societies in question, which systematically favour men over women – this is what is meant when discussing patriarchal societies. The documented practices include abortion of female foetuses (after mothers are advised they are carrying girls), and female infanticide (smothering or poisoning at birth). There is also the systematic and selective favouring of boys with regard to food, education, and healthcare (if there's not enough to go around, it's the boys who get whatever there is), which results in higher mortality rates for girls (see Ritchie and Roser 2019). It could also be that girls are not considered sufficiently important to count in official figures or that births of girl babies are hidden where there is compulsory restriction of family size. All these result from the relative powerlessness of women in relation to men; an issue important in explaining why HIV/AIDS is a heterosexual epidemic in Africa, as we saw earlier. In other words, the gender ratio is a social phenomenon. The quest for sociological explanation involves invoking an historical, cultural, and structural sensibility to explore how it results from the social organisation of the societies in question.

'*How could it be otherwise?*' This is the classic question asked as part of a critical sensibility. What alternative futures are there for young women growing up in these countries? How can the relative neglect of females in these societies be overcome? An exception to the pattern outlined above is the key to answering that question. The Indian state of Kerala is one of the poorest on the sub-continent, yet it has a female to male gender ratio of 104:100. Kerala also has the most developed school system in India (over 90 per cent of the population are literate), as well as a highly developed and extensive healthcare system. For the Nairs, one of the major ethnic groups that comprise Kerala society, property inheritance passes through the female line (Sen 1992: 587). The consequence of this is that the gender ratio more closely approximates the sex ratio.

The second example is that of Kenyan athletes. Why have Kenyan male athletes dominated middle- and long-distance running at Olympic Games? What combination of social and biological factors result in such success? In our local sports store there is a series of huge posters advertising a brand of sporting footwear with the theme, 'In my mind I am a Kenyan'. And Kenyans have been successful; since the 1960 Olympic Games in Rome, in the middle- and long-distance track races for men (800 metres to 10,000 metres), athletes from this small African country (nowadays sometimes running for other countries) have won an astonishing 70 medals. The next highest tally is 23 won by athletes from Ethiopia, followed by 16 from Great Britain, then Morocco with 10, and New Zealand with 9 (http: theolym picdatabase.nl/).

How has this country of 53 million people in 2020, one of the poorest countries in the world, with a Gross National Product per head ranked 155th in the world at $US1750 in 2019, managed to produce so many fine athletes? Ineffective drug testing regimes may well be a factor but Kenya is not alone in that problem. What is the relative importance of nature and nurture in explaining one of the major features of world track competition in recent decades?

Some biological factors, such as race, may be partially responsible. African and African-American athletes dominate world track and field in general, and in particular African-American athletes dominate the sprinting events. In the 2020 Tokyo Olympics only 5 of a possible 33 medals were won by athletes of Caucasian racial background in all men's track events up to the marathon, excluding the relays. It appears white men can't run (or jump!) though there are likely to be cultural factors at work here too.

A second factor in the terrain of biology is the well-known physiological effects of training at altitude. With a sizeable portion of Kenya more than 1,000 metres above sea level, the beneficial effects of growing up and training at higher altitudes are reflected in enhanced performances at sea level. Yet these aspects of explanation are only partial. Why would the biological advantage be bestowed on Kenyan athletes, and why not on the athletes of surrounding countries, such as Tanzania, Zaire, or Nigeria? Many other countries have high altitude areas but have not produced world-class athletes; for example, Nepal. Most importantly, though, if these biophysiological factors are so important, why do they only benefit men? Do Kenyan women somehow miss out on the advantage for running fast? The first medal (a silver) ever to be won by a female Kenyan track-and-field athlete occurred only at the Atlanta Olympics in 1996. Only since the Beijing Olympics in 2008 did Kenyan women begin to emulate their illustrious male counterparts and now have 20 track medals. It is therefore necessary to consider the social world to begin a sociological quest for explanation.

The four sociological sensibilities are important here. *Historically*, Kenya has links through colonialism with Great Britain, and a British tradition of athletics was imported into the schooling system from the early days. A similar argument would hold for the relative success of New Zealand in these events. This formed a culture in which athletics, rather than basketball or baseball, was a favoured sporting activity for athletically gifted youngsters. *Culturally* there is the importance of role models and imitation. When the sporting heroes of the country are athletes, all kids want to emulate them and win at those races; the races in which the sporting heroes excel on the international stage are the most prestigious ones (such as the sprints or middle-distance events). A part of the socialisation of young males appears to be idolisation of national sporting heroes. A parallel Australian example is cricket. When fast bowlers Glen McGrath and Dennis Lillee before him were the pin-up boys of Australian cricket, kids everywhere wanted to be fast bowlers and you would see them marking out huge run-ups halfway to the boundary and tearing in. But when spinner Shane Warne became the cricket hero, many kids wanted to be a spin bowler and the run-ups shortened dramatically! Lots of young boys want to be like English footballer Harry Kane, or All Blacks rugby player Beauden Barrett. Thus it is easy to see how a talented young Kenyan sportsman might decide to concentrate on middle-distance running rather than some other distance or some other sport. Similarly you would expect a talented young African-American or African-Canadian to concentrate on sprinting events. Imitation of those sports and events in which their country has major world presence is only to be expected.

Structural factors to do with the organisation of society are also relevant. Being a poor country, with a poorly developed transport infrastructure, including few school buses, it is common for young Kenyans to walk and run long distances to and from school, in effect training from an early age. Then there is considerable money to be made from athletics, especially from road races in affluent countries. Success in the international arena is a means of social mobility in monetary terms as well as status, with national and international recognition.

In addition, like many societies, preference may be given to boys rather than girls in the encouragement to pursue sporting activities; a result of a society structured in such a way that an unequal share of resources is accorded to men over women, in the manner argued in the example of the 'missing' women above. The behavioural expectations for young women, what are termed the 'social mores', mean that Kenyan women of child-bearing age have traditionally been expected to drop out of running and have children.

A contemporary layer to the problem of biology, gender, and athletics is the place of intersex and transgender athletes. A poignant example is that of the South African athlete Caster

Semenya (see Loland 2020). Semenya is an intersex woman with naturally elevated testosterone levels. The societal reactions to the participation and achievements of these athletes have covered a broad emotional spectrum from celebratory to claims that trans and intersex women athletes are erasing women's sport (*New York Times* 2020). There are also a number of athletes who have transitioned from male to female in recent times, often dominating female competition. The New Zealand weightlifter Laurel Hubbard became the first ever transgender athlete picked to compete at an Olympics in 2021 (Culpepper 2021). The biological dimensions of transitioning and competing aside, how does the social world mediate an otherwise straight-forward human activity such as playing sport? In the wider societal sphere, the issue of which public toilets people who identify as transgender or non-binary should use, has been controversial in many countries (see Forth 2021).

A *critical* sensibility asks, '*How could it be otherwise?*' For instance, how might Kenyan women be able to take advantage of the favourable environment towards athletics so as to emulate their male counterparts? Some of this is already occurring with several world-ranked Kenyan juniors among women athletes, and more Olympic medals as mentioned. Note the emphasis here is not only on how young Kenyan women might be encouraged to pursue athletics – in other words, by better individual adjustment to existing social and cultural conditions – but also how Kenyan society might facilitate greater participation of women athletes. All these sociological issues would need to be taken into account to complement the biologically based ones in order to develop an adequate explanation for this remarkable sporting achievement.

The boundary between the social world and the natural world is not rigidly drawn: the sociological quest involves carefully investigating where the boundary lies. A critical sensibility involves asking, '*How do you know?*' and our sociological BS detector is in regular use. In particular, it involves an awareness or sensitivity to explanations for social phenomena being made on biological grounds ('but it's only natural'). The implications of such an explanation is that this is the only possible order of things; that being based on biology or genetics, the existing social order is somehow fixed, immutable, and unchangeable. Asking, '*How could it be otherwise?*', involves a sensitivity to the possibilities for change and to alternative futures.

Investigating the boundary between biology and culture is also important when the issues appear to be mainly social. Let's consider as an example a major social policy decision being faced in the Australian context: What would be an appropriate size for the population of this country by the middle of the current century? How many more people than the current 25 million would be an appropriate level? Should it be a minimal increase to perhaps 30 million by the year 2050, or would 40 or maybe 50 million be an appropriate target? All of these have been suggested in recent debates, as the question of migration levels has become highly politicised.

The social policy question has been cast primarily in social terms because the rate of natural increase (from births) is likely to make a minimal impact on future population growth. Instead the level of immigration from other countries is likely to determine the population level. What should the migrant intake be? Given the large numbers of actual and potential trouble spots in the world, the misery of displaced people from around the world portrayed nightly on our television screens, the huge numbers of refugees seeking new homes, let alone vast numbers in other poorer countries who might choose to migrate to countries such as Australia should the opportunity arise, what policies should be pursued by governments?

The planning question clearly hinges in a considerable way on the implications of another 3, 8, or 33 million people. What would be the implications even of the modest increase to say 30 million by the year 2050? Given the clearly expressed historical preference for Australians, recently arrived or otherwise, to live 'between the desert and the beach', and particularly in urban areas near the coastline, what would be the implications of another two or three cities the size of Sydney or Melbourne? Would the additional population provide larger domestic markets, and therefore be likely to enhance the standard of living and quality of life for all Australians, as some economists claim? Or, given the current difficulty of providing employment for all those who require it, would these problems be compounded by another 8 million people? What would be the implications for some notion of social cohesion of Australia as a nation of such a population increase? Would one likely implication be the decline of the urban core as has occurred in the United States, another major country in the world built upon immigration? Would the implication be that some Australian cities may become like some of the most dangerous American cities, such as Washington, Los Angeles, and New York?

The social side of the question is also not the whole story. Environmental considerations such as climate change involve not only social aspects but also those concerned with water, air quality, and so on, which are also likely to influence decisions about the ability to sustain population increases on what is, after all, the driest continent as climate change in the direction of global warming tightens its grip. Although countries such as Australia have a low density of population by world standards, much of the continent is unsuitable or only marginally suitable for settlement. More than 200 years of white settlement of the continent has shown that clearly. The toll on the environment, on water, air, and forests, of even another 5 million, let alone another 8 or 33 million, is likely to be significant. Already attempts to increase agricultural production have resulted in significant environmental degradation in the form of rising salination, deforestation, the fouling and destruction of waterways, and the like. So, social planning questions about Australia's future will increasingly take these issues into account. As Furze (2008) argues, environmental problems are at their base social problems. So, environmental considerations combining both the social and biological will determine the outcome of the question of alternative futures in population size at the level of political process.

The boundary between the biological and the social world, between nature and culture, is a complex one, and one that is not easy to specify. Recent developments in Sociology are concerned with *deconstructing* the divide; that is, showing how the relationship is a complex one in which the categories themselves (such as nature/culture or sex/gender) are not easily defined or separated (see Turner 1992).

Biological determinism and ideology

The debate about the relative importance of the social and the biological has broader dimensions that require the exercising of the sociological sensibilities. In human history, the idea that biology is destiny has been a very powerful one. It is called *biological determinism* because it involves the idea that your biology at birth (black/white, male/female) will decide your chances in life. In other words, it accords a primary role for *ascribed status* (the personal characteristics you are born with) rather than *achieved status* (what you make of your life). It is an ideology in the sense that it is a set of ideas that justify a course of action.

This ideology of biological determinism has been called 'Social Darwinism'. It took Darwin's basic idea about 'survival of the fittest' and applied it to human societies (see Rose et al. 1984). According to this ideology, those who were 'fittest' were obviously those who had 'done best' by the contemporary criteria for assessing success in a society. Those who did not 'make it' were obviously less well equipped on the terrain of biology to 'succeed'. This ideology has been a powerful one, serving to *legitimate* (make seem right and proper) existing power structures and inequality, especially those based upon racism and sexism (see Gould 1981). Unequal opportunities for men and women that exist are often 'explained' in terms of female biology. In tennis, for example, the difference in the prize money at stake between the men's and women's finals in many of the world's leading tennis tournaments is 'explained' in terms of the frailness of women in playing only best of three instead of best of five sets. In other words, the social is reduced to the biological to make aspects of inequalities seem 'natural' and therefore inevitable. Only in 2007 did the organisers of the last of the four major tennis 'Grand Slam' events, Wimbledon, after considerable social pressure, pay equal prize money to the winners of the men's and women's singles (see Altius Directory 2010). In other countries, however, the disparity continues. In the Dubai Tennis

Championships in 2022, the winner of the women's singles received just 20 per cent of the prize money of the men's singles champion (Roberts 2022).

In today's society, the ideology of biological determination underlies theories and debates such as those suggesting a link between race and measures of intelligence. Invoking biological determinism legitimates exclusion policies. These policies include cuts in the taxes that attempt to ameliorate the effects of a market economy to maintain social cohesion, the abolition of social welfare programmes, and the abandoning of various affirmative action employment programmes, as well as the tightening of immigration requirements. Social control, not social amelioration, becomes the primary objective.

On the other hand, progressive social policies have attempted to challenge some of the effects of the ideology of biological determinism; to seek to make achieved status rather than ascribed status the basis for the distribution of social rewards in society as a means of trying to maximise human potentiality. Inclusive social policies have attempted to bring groups who may be marginal into the mainstream of society. The Civil Rights Act in the United States, the abolition of apartheid in South Africa, voting rights to First Nations Australians, and various affirmative action programmes were important moves in this direction. Many marginalised peoples are now able to live, marry, and seek the jobs they want, while these choices were previously banned to them on the basis of the ascribed characteristic of race.

Historically, however, the trend throughout much of the world, including Western countries, is towards inequalities being magnified and entrenched with considerable implications for the social cohesion and political stability of a society. One effect is with the political process where large swings in voter preferences, especially towards ultraconservative parties, have been a feature of the political landscape. In the context of structural change to the economies of societies through globalisation, the 'politics of blame' has led to an unfortunate process of scapegoating on racial grounds (First Nations people, recently arrived migrants), a form of biological determinism.

Conclusion

The quest for sociological understanding involves attention to the four features of explanation outlined in this book. One of the important ways in which such a sociological imagination can be used is to push back the conventionally held notions of the boundary between the natural and the social world. It is an ongoing debate, with new developments occurring all the time. For example, exciting possibilities are on the horizon, such as the elimination of some genetic diseases. A sociological imagination, however, is important to balance this debate. Our sociological BS detector remains important, particularly when explanations about the biological terrain for social phenomena begin to be used as a rationale for social and political programmes that accept the status quo as inevitable or somehow 'natural', and therefore immutable. The sense of critique and the search for alternative futures remain central to the sociological quest.

References

Altius Directory, 2010. [www.altiusdirectory.com/Sports/2010-wimble don-tennis-prize-money.php].

Bongaarts, J., and Guilmoto, C., 2015. 'How Many More Missing Women? Excess Female Mortality and Prenatal Sex Selection, 1970–2050', *Population and Development Review*, 41:2, 241–269.

Culpepper, C., 2021. 'Laurel Hubbard makes Olympic history as a transgender athlete', *Washington Post*, 2 August [www.washingtonp ost.com/sports/olympics/2021/08/02/laurel-hubbard-transgender-olympics-weightlifter].

Forth, Z., 2021. 'Not fitting into the gender binary makes public washrooms my enemy', Canadian Broadcasting Commission, 15 June [www.cbc.ca/news/canada/saskatoon/gendered-bathrooms-first-person-1.6058277].

Furze, B., 2008. 'Environmental Sustainability'. In Furze, B., Savy, P., Brym, R., and Lie, J. (eds), *Sociology in Today's World*. Cengage, Melbourne, 538–557.

Gould, S., 1981. *The Mismeasure of Man*. Norton, New York.

Hubbard, R., and Wald, E., 1993. *Exploding the Gene Myth*. Beacon Press, Boston.

Loland, S.J., 2020. 'Caster Semenya, Athlete Classification, and Fair Equality of Opportunity in Sport', *J Med Ethics*, 46:9, 584–590. doi:10.1136/medethics-2019-105937

New York Times (newspaper), 2020. 'Transgender athletes focus of debate on women's sports participants', *New York Times* (nytimes.com) Olympic Database [www.theolympicdatabase.nl/home].

Ritchie, H., and Roser, M., 2019. 'Gender ratio'. OurWorldInData.org. [https://ourworldindata.org/gender-ratio].

Roberts, O., 2022. 'Dubai tennis championships: prize money disparity highlights gender inequality', Give me Sport website, 22 February [www.givemesport.com/87975768-dubai-tennis-championships-prize-money-disparity-highlights-gender-inequality].

Rose, S., Lewontin, R., and Kamin, L., 1984. *Not in Our Genes: Biology, Ideology and Human Nature*. Penguin, London.

Sen, A., 1990. 'More than 100 million women are missing', *New York Review*, 20 December [www.nybooks.com/articles/1990/12/20/more-than-100-million-women-are-missing/].

—— 1992. 'Missing Women: Social Inequality Outweighs Women's Survival Advantage in Asia and North Africa', *British Medical Journal*, 304, March, 587–588.

Turner, B., 1992. *Regulating Bodies: Essays in Medical Sociology*, Routledge, London.

7 Theory and method

Having an historical, cultural, structural, and critical sensibility is crucial to the sociological quest. Now we can consider exactly how the insights generated by those sensibilities can be used in social analysis. This will be addressed by introducing the idea of sociological theories or perspectives, each with their own way of conceptualising the relationships. The links between theory and research will also be considered; that is, how we actually *do* Sociology.

Doing Sociology

Students who come to Sociology are often dismayed by the apparent lack of agreement between Sociologists on how the sociological quest should proceed and, at times, even what constitutes the discipline. Not all Sociologists would agree with the introduction to the discipline that this book represents. Some writers find it more appropriate to talk about 'sociologies' than Sociology (for example, Austin, 1984; Burawoy 2005). This is sometimes called the 'untidy face' of Sociology and is another way of saying there is no single body of knowledge, theories, or methods common to all Sociologists. Actually, the lack of theoretical agreement is a sign of a living, evolving discipline, which thrives on lively debates, not only over different theories but also over different methods, conflicting findings and the quality of evidence. The caricature that we have heard is that 'you ask two Sociologists for their view on something and you get ten

DOI: 10.4324/9781003316329-7

different opinions!' What exists is a collection of different ways of thinking that are variously called perspectives, approaches, theories, schools of thought, or traditions.

The perspective or theoretical approach affects the conduct of research when we come to make sociological explanations. For many, if not most, Sociologists the hallmark of a sociological way of approaching social phenomena is the concern with the integration of theory and method; integration in the sense of each being moulded and shaped by the other. The theoretical approach taken determines, to a considerable extent, the conduct of subsequent social research since the different perspectives generate certain sorts of research problems, which in turn favour certain sorts of methods for doing research.

On theory

What is a theory? *Theory* is a central element of all academic disciplines and all sciences. A theory is a statement that explains the nature of a relationship between concepts or ideas. Earlier we considered a theory about the relationship between external threat and internal solidarity in a society. Theory is necessary to begin to make sense of the 'facts'; that is, to interpret and give them meaning. Sometimes a distinction is drawn between theory, which is assumed to be somehow the 'ivory tower', and practice, which is more concrete and more useful. Behind every practical course of action, however, lies a theoretical basis for it. Often, spelling out the theory involves detailing the implicit bases or principles that make 'the facts' intelligible. Both theory and practice are closely related and both are important to the sociological quest.

In the early chapters, Sociology was defined as a social science involving a quest for explanations based on a rational appeal to impartial evidence. This chapter considers the nature of different sorts of explanations and the issue of evidence and how we 'know' things about the social world. The term used for this questioning of how we know things is 'epistemology'. An example of an epistemological question is if we are asked how I know what the meaning is of someone, say, gesturing towards someone else with their middle finger held upwards! This is to recall the infamous incident on a trip to Australia when the then president of the United States, on departing from an official function, gave what he assumed was a victory sign to his hosts! Considering these questions will demonstrate how the foundations of Sociology lie within philosophy, and the differences between the major socio-logical perspectives have their origins within the discipline of philosophy.

Method is used here to refer to the process of collecting information or data about the social world. The commonplace conception of the primary sociological method is the question-naire – a series of written questions asked of the respondent by the interviewer, either in person or by mail, phone, email, or on the internet. But there are many other ways of answering the question, 'How do you know?' We 'know' about the social world by conducting empirical research on some aspect or aspects of it. Asking some questions rather than others will affect the sort of information collected and the sorts of findings likely to be made. Theory, method, and findings or results shape and mould each other. The important point is that information or data about the social world does not exist in some free-floating, independent way. Instead it exists as the answer to a sociological question or problem which makes its gathering and interpretation rele-vant. Another way of saying this is that a concern with the unity of theory and method is central to the quest for sociological understanding.

This concern with the unity of theory and method is often used to differentiate Sociology from journalism, the latter usually being concerned with more immediate aspects of social issues and not with the underlying theoretical aspects of the process of knowing about the social world. Different theories have different means of approaching social phenomena, but their unifying fea-ture, and indeed the feature which gives the discipline its defining characteristic and coherence, is the issue of the place of the indi-vidual in the larger scheme of things. How is it that despite our individuality, our unique experiences and our differences, we all manage to behave socially and be part of a collective entity known as a society?

In discussing the main perspectives of the discipline, there are some aspects to bear in mind. First, there is no fixed, uniformly agreed upon idea of what the major perspectives are. They are called different names by different Sociologists, and there is disagreement on the extent to which the different perspectives overlap. What is presented below in more detail as the three main perspectives of classical Sociology – functionalism, conflict theory, and interactionism – would be agreed upon by probably most, but by no means all, Sociologists. Within each there is a variety of different approaches and differences between the approaches, which result from different historical, geographical, and social circumstances. What is presented here is an attempt to classify these approaches, to illustrate them. As you delve further into the study of the discipline of Sociology, you will be introduced to more contemporary perspectives that critique some or all of these classical perspectives. Some of these contemporary perspectives for studying society include postmodernism, poststructuralism, feminist theory, and cultural studies. For now, however, we have taken the approach of introducing a fairly conventional understanding of the sociological imagination, as a building block upon which, and against which, other theoretical approaches can be developed in any further studies the reader may take in Sociology.

Second, while all Sociologists work to a greater or lesser extent within certain perspectives, they do not go around wearing badges identifying what their preferred perspective is. To some extent at least, it is possible to draw on more than one perspective in seeking to understand and analyse a particular sociological problem. Third, having a perspective is unavoidable. In order to focus our attention to even begin to make sense of something, we need some selectivity. So there is no such thing as a perspectiveless sociological account. There are only differing degrees of implicitness and explicitness of that perspective. This point applies to all academic disciplines, including the natural and physical sciences, not just to Sociology.

In some sciences though, the perspective or *paradigm*, as it is sometimes called, is accepted to the point where it is taken for granted. Astronomy, for instance, operates with a heliocentric perspective of the universe. The sun is at the centre of the solar system and the planets revolve around it. Yet until Copernicus showed this to be the case in the sixteenth century, astronomy was based on the geocentric paradigm proposed by Ptolemy, where the Earth was held to be at the centre of the universe. Likewise in medicine: the late nineteenth and early twentieth centuries are marked by the gradual rise to dominance of the so-called 'germ theory' of disease. Different perspectives or theories of disease are followed by the modalities of so-called 'alternative medicine', such as chiropractic, naturopathy, and homoeopathy. All these are theories of the causation of ill health in the sense that they are statements about the relationship between health and other factors.

So what are these sociological perspectives? At their most elementary, they are simply a point of view. More than that, however, they may be defined as a relatively coherent tradition of ideas about the world and how it works. In Sociology they tend to go by the name either of the major person who was responsible for giving coherence to the perspective as we know it today, or of the major idea they encompass. While they all propose a way of studying the relationship between the individual and society, they differ in two main ways. First, they make mutually incompatible philosophical assumptions about the objects of study, the nature of the individual and of society, and the relationship between the two. Second, they disagree about the meaning and validity of the knowledge derived from the particular perspectives; that is, on the status of the knowledge derived from the particular perspectives. We will deal with this point later in the chapter to stress the link between the perspective taken and the method adopted for studying the social world.

The underlying assumptions

One of the bases on which the perspectives can be differentiated is by the positions they take on the major philosophical debates which underlie the social sciences. (Our aim here is to introduce the sociological representations of some major philosophical issues and debates.) These positions take the form of assumptions in the sense of not being empirically testable but existing at the philosophical level. These assumptions tend to be dualistic; that is, the debates are presented as contrasting pairs with each perspective taking a position in relation to one side or the other. Mostly they can be represented as a continuum in which one takes a position at one end or the other. It should be remembered that our treatment of these issues only scratches the surface of the substantial debates in the philosophy of the social sciences, but it gives some basis for understanding how the major perspectives of Sociology differ from other disciplines.

The first set of these assumptions concerns the *nature of the individual*. This is basically a set of assumptions about human nature. Is human nature more self-centred or altruistic, more competitive or cooperative, more rational or irrational? These are basically untestable propositions about which one makes assumptions. To put it another way, the question, 'What is human nature?', is not empirically resolvable. The two basic philosophical positions are Thomas Hobbes' (philosopher, 1588–1679) pessimistic view of human nature and the more optimistic position espoused by Jean Jacques Rousseau (philosopher, 1712–78). When Anne Frank wrote in her diary near the end of her time in hiding from the Nazis in wartime Amsterdam, and near the subsequent end of her life in a concentration camp, 'In spite of everything, I still believe people are really good at heart', she was taking a clear Rousseauean position. If she had, perhaps understandably, come to the view of the inherent evilness of the occupying Nazis, she would have been taking a more Hobbesian position.

The *nature of society* is the second set of assumptions. One debate here is whether society exists only in human consciousness (the subjectivist position), or whether it has an independent existence (the objectivist position). The terms 'objective' and 'subjective' are not used here in their commonsense meanings, concerning whether one's values are involved or not. Rather, this huge philosophical debate revolves around the question of the nature of reality. One nice example to illustrate this debate is how it has come to light that up-market clothing stores, in a marketing strategy aimed at flattery to improve sales, are resizing women's clothes. Clothes that had carried a size 12 label are now being labelled size 10, what many regard (historically and culturally) as the ideal body size. Size 14 clothes are likewise being relabelled size 12, and so on. One chain in particular, selling clothes under the Country Road label, has applied for the change to be recognised officially by the relevant government standards authority that defines the sizes; that is, what configuration of hip, waist, and bust measurements objectively constitutes which size. The authority has indicated there will be no change in official sizing measurements. Its position is an objectivist one – there is an objective reality in which certain measurements 'mean' size 10. The clothing chain, by contrast, is operating with a subjectivist position on clothing sizes, socially constructing the meaning of size 10 in the hope that sales will be improved by more women fitting clothes with a label indicating small-sized clothes.

In other countries the sizing of clothes is even more confusing. In the United States, for instance, while men's clothing sizes tend to be standard (a certain combination of waist, chest, and neck size 'objectively means' a particular clothing size), for women the situation is more complex. There exists no industry-wide sizing standards in the US$1.5 trillion annual apparel market. There appears to be no similar uniform objectivist measurements of what combination of hip, waist, and bust measurement means what size. The result is that buying clothes is much more complex (and organised on a subjectivist basis) because you might require a particular size of clothing in one shop and another size elsewhere.

Arguing a subjectivist position on the nature of society would indicate that people construct in their minds an entity called 'Australian society', 'American society', 'British society', or 'New Zealand society', helped along by symbols which represent the entity, such as flags, national anthems, totems, or particular colour combinations, be they green and gold, red, white, and blue, or black and white. Related to this is the debate about whether society is more than the sum of its individual parts or just the sum of the individuals who comprise it. Already the reader may be able to see some of the positions we have taken so far in this book. Earlier we made the argument that society is more than the sum of its parts. This is in the same way that a cake cannot be considered to be just the sum of its ingredients – the act of cooking (or by analogy, living in society) modifies some of the individualistic elements.

A third assumption is the *nature of social change*, about whether change in society occurs because of an evolutionary or revolutionary basis. Evolutionary social change is gradual, incremental, and small-scale. Revolutionary social change, by contrast, is more large scale. Should the major changes occurring in our society associated with globalisation and the restructuring of the economy in the name of the ideologies of 'compete or perish' and 'level playing fields' be considered evolutionary or revolutionary social change? Should the events that have occurred in Afghanistan, the Middle East, or Eastern Europe be considered evolutionary or revolutionary?

Likewise, should we regard smaller scale changes in the way our society operates as evolutionary or revolutionary? Think of changes in the social acceptability of smoking, particularly in public places. Or perhaps the variable extent of changes among Caucasians in culturally valued body colouring – from tanned to what has been called a 'peaches and cream' complexion – associated with concerns about skin cancer. Do these changes follow from earlier changes or are they of a markedly different nature?

Another related set of assumptions concerns *the relationship between the individual and society*. First among these is the debate over the basis for the social order. How does the society in which we live manage to exist and survive over time? One answer is on the basis of consensus: we basically have shared values and agree on what is necessary for social order to continue. The sanctity of human life and property is one of these shared values. The other position is that social order is only possible on the basis of coercion. Conflict occurs between groups in society with different values, in which more powerful social groups impose their will over and control less powerful groups. This is the basis of social order. The sanctity of human life and property is maintained by a large and active police presence. Those who benefit most from the value of the sanctity of property are those who have most of it.

The second assumption made about the relationship between the individual and society arises out of the major philosophical debate about the extent of *determinism and free will* in the conduct of human affairs. There are various types of determinism; here we are only concerned with the question in a broad context. To what extent do the expectations of others and of the society as a whole determine our individual actions, or do we have free will to decide for ourselves? A major decision commonly faced by young people in establishing an adult identity is whether they will formalise their principal emotional and sexual relationship by actually getting married. Will they respond to the frequent expectations of others, such as parents, by actually 'tying the knot'? To take a position at one end of this continuum is to argue that we are determined to a greater or lesser extent by the expectations others have of us. To take a position at the other end of the continuum is to argue that we have free will to choose to respond to those expectations or to ignore them.

A French school of philosophy known as existentialism, whose principal figure was Jean-Paul Sartre, takes the position at the pole of the continuum. Individuals always have choice and free will to decide their actions. So you can never say as a way of being released from responsibility for your actions that you had no choice. You are acting in 'bad faith' (that is, deceiving yourself) if you do. Lest you think of this as an esoteric debate with little relevance, it was the basis for the Nuremberg trials, one of the most important legal events of the last century. The basis on which the Nazi defendants were prosecuted as war criminals and on which a number of them were executed was the disallowing of what has come to be called the Eichmann defence: they were just following orders. The case against them was based on the argument that they had free will. Indeed, if enough had refused to follow orders the war crimes would not have occurred.

A sociological representation of this philosophical debate is the distinction outlined in a previous chapter between agency and structure. The question revolves around whether people produce society or are determined by it; the role of individual human agency as against the constraints and determinants of action arising from the expectations of others. This theme is explored extensively in the classic introduction to the discipline by Peter Berger (1963).

The other major philosophical debate for our purposes here is that which requires assumptions to be made between *materialism and idealism*. The use of these terms has nothing to do with their commonsense association with one being materialistic or idealistic. Rather, the debate refers to what has priority, what comes first: people's material existence or their ideas. The famous quote from Karl Marx that social being determines consciousness epitomises the materialist position. For Marx, the position you hold in society (expressed as your class position) will determine your ideas about the world. From an idealist position, the reverse is argued; the ideas people hold will affect their social location (as we saw earlier with Max Weber's ideas about economic change). So it is possible to have materialist and idealist strategies of social change. For Marx this involved the extreme lengths of changing the economic basis on which society operated. Idealist solutions rely more on educating people differently, that is, changing their ideas.

The three major perspectives

Having considered very briefly the main underlying philosophical debates that together provide one basis for differentiating between theoretical perspectives, the three major traditional perspectives of Sociology in terms of the positions they take on these debates about the individual and society will now be outlined. These perspectives are commonly known as *functionalism*, *conflict theory*, and *interactionism*. Outlined here is one quite common characterisation of the complexity of perspectives. Many other perspectives exist, but most are variations to a greater or lesser extent of these major three. Only the main points will be outlined here; all have been subjected to much critical examination, which can be studied elsewhere (see, for instance, Cuff et al. 1990).

Functionalism

This perspective is also referred to as 'the society perspective' or the 'social system perspective'. It is a tradition of sociological thought that derives from the work of the French sociologist, Emile Durkheim, although it was principally given coherence by the American, Talcott Parsons (1902–79). In the early stages of the development of the discipline, in the 1940s to 1960s, and particularly in the United States, it approximated a position of dominance. Today, following sustained criticism, there are few adherents amongst professional Sociologists, but its importance lies in the enduring relevance of some aspects of the insights it generates and also in the similarities it shares with much commonsense thinking about social issues. It is for this reason, as Margaret Sargant (1983) puts it, that 'Talcott Parsons is dug up and reburied each year'.

Of the individual, the assumptions are pessimistic. Basic human nature is said to be self-centred and irrational. Society, then, acts as a civilising influence to make social order stable, orderly, and harmonious; in effect preventing a Hobbesian 'war of all against all'. Society is more than the sum of its parts and confronts individuals as an objective reality. The relationship between the individual and society is then cast as a tension. The civilising influence of society keeps irrationality in check, with individuals not actively creating social lives but products of the external society (as we saw with the example of Norbert Elias' theory of the civilising process). Individuals can then only be free and happy within the confines set up by society. In this perspective there is an assumption of consensus on the basis of a shared system of values. This underlying assumption gives rise to statements such as, 'It's in the national interest', where there is assumed to be no conflict of interest. Social change is assumed to be only of a very gradual, evolutionary kind.

Within this perspective, *roles* provide the link between the individual and society in a fairly determinist fashion. As individuals we are linked to the various institutions of society by filling roles. At home, in the institution of kinship, we fill the roles of child or parent. At work, employer and employee. In the education system, pupil and teacher. In the health system, patient and health practitioner. Interaction between individuals is stabilised on the basis of a common value system; we agree on what should happen ('You want to get well, don't you?'). Conflict that may occur is to be understood as poor role performance. Divorce, for example, occurs because the partners are not fulfilling role requirements of husbands and wives adequately. In this perspective the process of *socialisation* is heavily emphasised. By being socialised, we learn to be social, to keep our basically irrational tendencies in check, and the content of role expectations. Divorce may also be caused by poor role socialisation. The solution is an idealist one: educate young people better on how to be good husbands or wives.

Functionalism also uses the concept of *social systems* as the central unit of analysis. These social systems can range in scope from a *dyad* (a two-person social system, such as parent–child, teacher–pupil) up to the society as a whole. The key sense of sociological problem of this perspective is to ask, 'What is the function of a particular component of society, for example, religion, the family, universities, etc., in maintaining social order and the continued existence of society?' Statements such as, 'Religion exists to sustain the moral foundations of society', are informed by this perspective. This is not the place to go into the drawbacks of the various perspectives, but it is important to note the assumption here is that society is *intended* to promote social order and integration.

The implication that 'society' can have a purpose or can be considered as an actor is called *reification*. In terms of logic, it should be noted it can result in a circular argument (called a *teleological* argument). In other words, our sociological BS detector should switch to red alert when we hear statements like, 'Society forces people to do...', or some reference to an unspecified 'they'. Statements like, 'Every society controls to a certain extent who may marry whom' (common in undergraduate essays), fail to consider who is actually doing the controlling or law making. The law makers and parliaments have decided you cannot marry your brother or sister, not some entity called society. Reification, while perhaps most common in functionalist accounts of social phenomena, is not restricted to that perspective, but is a more general alert. It occurs, for instance, whenever the term 'unAustralian' is used, which regrettably seems to be occurring with increasing frequency in present political debate. Indeed the respected social commentator Hugh McKay refers to it as 'an ugly word and a signpost to an ugly trend' (McKay 2005).

Conflict theories

This tradition may be understood as a set of theories and its most important figure is Karl Marx (1818–83), though many others are also involved. In discussing Marx's work we are separating (in a way Marx himself would have staunchly opposed) his analysis of society from his particular prescription of what should and would happen to change that society. Marx's work remains important to the social sciences despite attempts to discredit its relevance because of the collapse of societies in Eastern Europe and elsewhere based (albeit only very loosely) on his ideas.

In terms of the assumptions, conflict theories (of which, as with the other perspectives, there are a number) have a positive, optimistic view of human nature, arguing that human nature has been perverted by social arrangements through most of history. Society, then, is seen not as a civilising influence – as with functionalist theories – but as a corrupting influence, in effect creating conditions under which individuals become greedy, exploitative, and uncooperative. In terms of the relationship between the individual and society, a key assumption is that conflict or coercion is the basis of a social order in which a minority of powerful people are able to impose their wills over the rest. (In the Marxian varieties of this perspective these groups of people are *classes*.) Unlike the functionalist perspective, then, conflict and conflicts of interest are a normal aspect of the way a society operates. Therefore, far from divorce being caused by poor role socialisation and performance, from this perspective, conflict is an endemic, normal part of a relationship. What happens, for instance, in a doctor's surgery is not assumed to be stabilised on the basis of shared values but may be the result of the patient and doctor sometimes having different outcome aims from the encounter. Rather than sharing the aim of getting well as quickly as possible, the patient may be more interested in securing a medical certificate to legitimate submitting an essay after the due date or getting time off work.

The relationship between the individual and society in this perspective is cast as a contradiction. People are the way they are because of the sort of society in which they live. Unlike functionalism, however, there exists the possibility that this contradiction can be resolved by changing the sort of society in which people live. Furthermore, this perspective makes a materialist assumption. The explanation for features of the society, such as inequality, conflict, change, unemployment, divorce, and so on, is to be sought in the way in which a particular society organises its economic life. The focus is on how economic production is organised. In the case of many countries the term given to this organisation is 'capitalism', based on private ownership of resources and the production of goods and services for profit.

Hence amongst the terms 'advanced', 'modern', 'Western', and 'capitalist', which are used to describe what sort of society we live in, the last mentioned is the most important. Conflict theories tend to make quite determinist assumptions (and are frequently criticised for doing so). They are determinist in the sense that it is assumed that much of the shape of our society and many of its features are, to a greater or lesser extent (there's a lot of argument here, too), the result of the fact that we live in a capitalist society. These features not only include how education, health, and other services are provided but also features such as the idea of fashionableness. What else would convince you it is time to spend some of your hard-earned money on new clothes when the ones you have are perfectly wearable – they are just not the new season's fashions!

The main differences between conflict theories and functionalism are the assumption of conflict in the former versus consensus in the latter, as well as how they view human nature and society. There are similarities, too: both are structural in orientation, articulating the relationship between the individual and society by beginning at the group level, then moving down to the individual level; both are objectivist in their view of society as having an independent existence; both are at least relatively determinist in focusing on society as a whole. The following example, however, should clarify how they differ and illustrate the implications of the different assumptions about the nature of the individual, of society, and of the relationship between the two.

Social media has given rise to a revolution in communications, providing profoundly democratic platforms for expression and social connection. While there are many pleasures and benefits to social media use, from the dopamine hit of a funny meme and the socially validating warmth derived from numerous 'likes' for achievements, to the viral awareness of social justice campaigns, there is also a pronounced dark side. Aside from the prolific personal abuse associated with social media use, one of the most concerning problems with this form of social interaction is the escalating rates of harm to mental health. While social relationships are critical to good mental health, aspects of their translation to social media formats has raised alarms with mental health practioners, particularly for young people and for young women especially (Forbes 2021). A major problem with social media among young people is the immense pressure to compete with friends and connections by posting only positive images and impressions of their lives, under-emphasising or omitting any negative experiences. The rise and rise of what's been called 'toxic positivity' (Bastion and Humphrey 2021) has had a significant impact on social interaction to the point where perfect online scripts are taken for reality, creating a sense of failure, shame, and crashing self esteem in those whose lives are not so great. A further insidious dimension to this phenomena is the hyper commercialisation of toxic positivity whereby 'influencers' are highly financially incentivised to perform and produce such lives online.

Two different ways of explaining such behaviour present themselves, related to the assumptions about the nature of the individual and society. One, functionalist in nature, would arise out of a pessimistic view of human nature, seeing the civilising effects of educating people in society as having failed to prevent such behaviour occurring. In other words, the primary responsibility for such behaviour lies at the individual level. The other way of understanding such behaviour, informed by conflict assumptions that are optimistic about human nature, would consider the way in which current social arrangements alienate and marginalise some groups of the population so that such behaviours may result. If young people, and young women in particular, do not actually live perfectly positive lives as determined by socially and culturally entrenched gendered expectations around youth, financial success, and positivity then they are more likely to produce an unrealistic attitude to the presentation of self to the rest of the community.

Since this is an aspect of the sociological imagination that is sometimes misunderstood, it is worth reiterating that holding the latter view does not absolve the people concerned from responsibility for their actions. Rather, it is to argue that we will not get far in stopping the practice by pursuing solely idealist (in the specific sociological sense of the term outlined earlier) solutions, by attempting to socialise and educate people not to engage in such practices. Instead, materialist solutions must also be pursued, such as secure meaningful employment diminishing the incentive to 'influence' on social media and other means of integrating a more accepting set of life images and experiences into the mainstream of social life from their position of the toxically positive.

Interactionism

As with conflict theories, this term refers to a tradition of theoretical approaches that have commonly arisen out of the microsociological work of the German sociologist Max Weber (1864–1920), although the approaches have been developed, particularly in the American context, by George Herbert Mead (1863–1931) and Alfred Schutz (1899–1959). Weber's work spans both conflict theory and interactionism but interactionists, such as Mead and Schutz, used some of his understandings to develop their own approaches. This perspective is sometimes known as 'social action theory'. With its primary focus on small-scale social phenomena, this perspective tends to make relativistic assumptions about the nature of the individual, society and the relationship between the two: that they will vary with time and circumstance and are not absolute as the more objectivist perspectives of functionalism and conflict theory assume.

With this perspective, people are active agents, creating and recreating society rather than acting in accordance with some external constraints. It assumes individuals actively interpret in the sense of making sense of themselves, others, and social and physical situations. From this perspective history has no grand design, either evolutionary or revolutionary. Events take place by the action of individuals collectively negotiating goals in the context of free will. Unlike the other perspectives there is little by way of a macro view of the world. Individuals act in terms of their interpretations to construct the group or societal level of interaction. As the sociological adage originating from the American sociologist W.I. Thomas states, 'That which is defined as real is real in its consequences', even in circumstances where those interpretations may be able to be demonstrated to be false. A neighbour of Evan's, for example, prefers not to paint his house too often as a means of discouraging burglars, hoping they will define the situation as, 'This is a house in which there is not likely to be much worth stealing'.

Interactionism, then, makes a subjectivist assumption that there is no absolute reality, but that people purposefully construct their social reality. The purpose is the goals they seek (such as not being burgled). Social action is assumed to be goal orientated. Individuals have free will to actively construct meaning in terms of their motivations.

This perspective is also idealist, according importance to ideas and values in the constructions of meaning that individuals make in their own right and not as derivative of some under-lying objective material reality. No common system of values is assumed, unlike functionalism. Rather, the emphasis is on diver-sity of values as individuals try to achieve their goals, which may be either in cooperation or in conflict with others. So inter-actionism makes different assumptions from either functionalism or conflict theory. In particular, it stresses free will rather than determinism and social life as subjective rather than objective reality. It shares with conflict theory the emphasis on conflict.

These perspectives represent the three main ways in which Sociologists have conceptualised the relationship between the individual and society, which then provides the basis for their research practice. The perspectives differ according to the assumptions they make about some of the key debates in the philosophy of the social sciences. The philosophical differences result in different ways of understanding the nature of the socio-logical quest and also have an impact on the sense of sociological problem that each perspective addresses. The differences between the perspectives and the effect of the different philosophical assumptions on the sense of sociological problem that results, which therefore affects the sort of research undertaken, can be illuminated with an example.

An example – the Sociology of death

The topic of death is perhaps not one that is obviously amenable to a sociological analysis, but from a sociological point of view we are interested in the fact that while the society as a whole continues to exist and survive over time, individual members 'turn up their toes' and pass out of that society. As indicated, functionalism concentrates on questions about the mainten-ance of a consensual social order. For Sociologists from this perspective then (for example, Blauner 1966), the sense of socio-logical problem that arises is how a society copes with the loss of individual members without the ongoing social order being unduly disrupted. The important question becomes, 'What is the function of death rituals, such as funerals, for the maintenance of social order?' The answer is that these rituals help to mark the passing of an individual and assist those remaining to resume their function in society. Likewise, the convention and, indeed until recently, the legal requirement of mandatory retirement at age 67 in most jobs is functional for society because it minimises the disruption to the normal working of the society occasioned by having members of the society dying while holding important economic roles in that society. Given that mandatory retirement has been challenged as discriminatory and ageist, the question from this point of view is, 'What will be the consequences for the maintenance of social order if this change occurs?' Will it be functional for society to have people working on into their sev-enth and even eighth decade?

From a conflict perspective, the sorts of sociological questions that are asked concern the way in which the arrangements to do with death are organised, which is the result of the sort of society we live in (for example, Marcuse 1972). Sociological accounts of death informed by a conflict perspective consider, for instance, the implications of the fact that we live in a capitalist society.

Attention has therefore focused on the funeral industry and the way in which profitability is pursued in the marketing of various services that funeral companies offer (such as the variable price of coffins). Alternatively, studies may focus on what has come to be called the *commodification* of human services, in this case in the area of death and dying. With this sense of problem, Sociologists find interesting, for instance, the Californian Yellow Pages® online, where the range of services advertised includes being able to employ a suitably trained person to undertake 'the death watch'. For a reasonably hefty hourly rate, this person will sit with your relative or friend in the last hours before their death. In other words, in California you can pay for something which traditionally has been regarded as one of the most important kinship obligations. This is part of a general process identified by Marx: as capitalism develops, the cash nexus increasingly comes to replace the notion of personalised service. It becomes a commodity like anything else, to be bought and sold.

From an interactionist perspective, the key sorts of sociological questions asked differ again. Accounts based on this perspective consider the way in which social action occurs as individual members of society imbue with meaning the death of one of their number. The focus here is not on the broader society and how it structures the experience of dying for individuals, but more upon smaller scale interaction within hospitals, funeral parlours, and so on. Operating from this perspective, Sociologists might consider the way a language has evolved which is 'deathless' ('passing on' rather than 'dying', 'deceased' rather than 'dead', 'interred' rather than 'buried', a 'floral tribute' rather than 'flowers'). Alternatively, they may consider the routines and procedures that have evolved in hospital settings to minimise the disruptive impact of individual patients dying (such as a special lift to the morgue to remove the need for visitors to share the lift with a corpse). Or they might study the different definitions of the situation held by health workers for whom death is routine and commonplace, and the rest of us for whom it is not. This tension is ably reflected in the supposedly true story of a medical student, who was very nearly expelled from medical school after he leant out of the window of an anatomy laboratory and inquired of the window cleaner working there whether he would like a hand! Alternatively, they may study, as Allan Kellehear (1990) did in his classic work in this field, the manner in which the notion of 'good death' is constructed.

Of course the sense of problem raised by all three perspectives are relevant sociological questions in understanding the phenomenon of death in society. The point is that the perspective from which the researcher operates will affect the sorts of sociological problems that are considered to be relevant, as well as how the researcher goes about investigating that phenomenon.

Several other points are relevant to the example of the different sociological perspectives on death used above. First, all sociological accounts are informed by perspectives. The unity of theory and method is what makes Sociology distinctive. It is not possible to have a perspectiveless account of social phenomena, only degrees of implicitness and explicitness. All sociological analysis operates from a particular perspective, in the sense of providing a basis from which analysis can proceed, even if that perspective is only implicit in the author's account. This relates to the argument in the previous chapter about the question of values, where it was argued that a value-free account was impossible. Even to decide what sorts of sociological questions to ask about a particular phenomenon requires taking some sort of position in relation to the underlying philosophical debates which inform the perspectives. Most Sociologists would argue that it is preferable to be reasonably explicit about the perspective from which one operates.

Second, it relates to the question of critique, which we have argued is an essential component of the quest for sociological understanding. One can be critical of another's account of an aspect of the social world in two ways: either in terms of the conventional criteria of the adequacy of the empirical evidence or data used to support the argument (which we shall deal with in the next chapter); or in terms of a different perspective taken to inform one's account of the particular topic. For instance, one might be critical of an interactionist account of the social processes that surround death on the (more structuralist) grounds that they fail to adequately take account of the broader context in which the services surrounding the death of an individual are organised on a business basis. Likewise, from an interactionist perspective, one may be critical of more structural accounts for failing to take adequate account of the interactional details and for assuming that what actually occurs will be determined by the broader societal level considerations.

Third, there is the often asked question of the extent to which one can mix the perspectives to suit the purpose in hand – sometimes called a *pluralist perspective*. The answer to this question has to be that it is possible to some extent. A sociological analysis of death is improved by taking into consideration the sorts of insights generated by all three perspectives outlined in the example above. The limitation on a sort of theoretical smorgasbord, however, comes from the underlying philosophical bases. The positions that are taken by the different perspectives are at times mutually incompatible. One cannot assume both an optimistic and pessimistic view of human nature. At a philosophical level they may be what is called *incommensurable*.

Finally, we can consider how the earlier chapters of this book relate to the idea of perspectives. How the sociological imagination, arising from exercising sensibilities towards the historical, cultural, structural, and critical aspects of sociological analysis, is incorporated into a sociological understanding, for instance, of death, will depend on the perspective taken. So, taking an historical sensibility as the example, if you operate within a functionalist perspective, then the relevant historical issues to consider will be the history of retirement policy or changes in the format of funerals, for example. If, however, your social analysis is informed by a conflict perspective, then the relevant historical questions will include the history of the funeral parlour industry, its origins as a sideline for furniture makers and the gradual emergence of it as a specialised service industry. Incorporating a cultural sensibility from a functionalist perspective will focus on how funeral rituals are performed in different cultures or how retirement policy is organised elsewhere. From a conflict perspective, the relevant question might be something like, 'Is the Californian example given above something specific to west-coast American culture, or is it a consequence of the more general process of commodification such that this service will eventually be able to be engaged in Wellington or Perth as well?' From an inter-actionist perspective, the appropriate question might be how to make practices surrounding the dead (in hospitals or funeral homes) more culturally sensitive to different ethnic groups, in line with their particular beliefs and customs. In other words, the quest for sociological understanding requires these sensibilities to be built into social analysis, but how and the extent to which it is done will depend to a considerable extent on the perspective taken.

Conclusion

This chapter considered the idea of perspectives within Sociology. These perspectives are sociological representations of the underlying philosophical debates of the social sciences. The three perspectives outlined – functionalism, conflict theory, and interactionism – represent the main theoretical traditions within which the sociological quest may proceed. Another way of saying this is that these are, to a greater or lesser extent, the main traditions within which Sociology is practised today. Flowing from the perspective taken will be a preference for certain methods of doing Sociology over others. In other words, there is a fundamental unity in the discipline between theory and method.

Sociological analysis, then, has as its fundamental feature a concern with relating the unobservable aspects of the social world to the observable. The unobservable is the social theory that underlies the discipline. The observable is evidence about the social world. Sociology cannot be practised without the existence of both.

References

Austin, D., 1984. *Australian Sociologies*. Allen and Unwin, Sydney.

Bastion, B., and Humphrey, A., 2021. 'How to avoid "toxic positivity" and take the less direct route to happiness', 31 October [https://theconversation.com/how-to-avoid-toxic-positivity-and-take-the-less-direct-route-to-happiness-170260].

Berger, P., 1963. *An Invitation to Sociology*. Penguin, New York.

Blauner, R., 1966. 'Death and the Social Structure', *Psychiatry*, 29:4, 378–394.

Burawoy, Michael, 2005. '2004 ASA Presidential Address – For Public Sociology', *American Sociological Review*, 70 (February): 4–28.

Cuff, E., Sharrock, W., and Francis, D., 1990, *Perspectives in Sociology*, 3rd edn. Unwin Hyman, London.

Forbes, 2021. 'Here's how Instagram harms young women according to research', 5 October [www.forbes.com/sites/kimelsesser/2021/10/05/heres-how-instagram-harms-young-women-according-to-resea rch/?sh=3e067250255a].

Kellehear, A., 1990. *Dying of Cancer*. Harwood, London.

Marcuse, H., 1972. *Eros and Civilisation*. Abacus, London.

McKay, H., 2005. 'Just who is un-Australian?' *The Age* (newspaper), 20 June [www.theage.com.au/opinion/just-who-is-un-australian-20050620-ge0dib.html].

Sargant, M., 1983. *Sociology for Australians*. Longman Cheshire, Melbourne.

8 How do we know?

As indicated in the previous chapter, the different perspectives can be differentiated in two main ways. The first is the assumptions they make in regard to key debates in the philosophy of the social sciences. The other is in terms of the answer given to the epistemological question of '*How can we know the social world?*' – that is, about the status of the knowledge to be derived from the various perspectives. The last section of this chapter will consider this question.

The perspective taken has implications for how we do Sociology and what we consider to be its subject matter. This is the link between the theoretical or non-observable aspects of the social world and the empirical or observable aspects. In other words, it is to discuss the relationship between concepts you cannot see (such as class), and those you can see (such as education levels). Empirical research about the social world does not occur in a vacuum; rather, it is conducted within a particular perspective. These relate closely to the approaches to the discipline itself outlined previously. There a distinction was drawn between the approach to the discipline usually called positivism, which sees Sociology as emulating the natural and physical sciences, and the non-positivist approach, sometimes called naturalism, which sees the social sciences as different from the natural and physical sciences and which therefore pursues the sociological quest differently. Having considered the underlying assumptions, we are now in a position to understand better the difference between

DOI: 10.4324/9781003316329-8

these two approaches to the nature of the discipline and then relate it to the perspectives outlined above.

The crucial assumption concerns the nature of reality. Objectivist approaches assume a definite social reality exists. Subjectivist approaches, by contrast, assume people give meaning to a social setting, and thus socially construct a reality. Positivist approaches assume an objectivist reality, therefore one can *know by measuring*. If a social reality exists out there, then the sociologist operating from this perspective can emulate their natural and physical science colleagues and take their version of the thermometer or the Geiger counter, which is most likely to be a questionnaire, into a particular social setting to know what is happening there; in other words, to research it. Sociologists operating within this positivist tradition therefore have a preference for what is usually called *quantitative* methods of gathering data over other methods.

Sociologists operating within the non-positivist tradition of doing Sociology, however, seek to know things about the social world in a different manner. Arising from a subjectivist assumption about the nature of reality, these Sociologists pursue their sociological quest by seeking to *know by interpreting or understanding*. If social reality is constructed by participants pursuing their goals, then the sociologist must try to tap into the meaning the participants give to the social settings of which they are a part. The epistemological process is called *verstehen* (pronounced 'ver-shtay-en'). This German word, coined by Max Weber, expresses an idea that cannot easily be translated into the English language. It means interpretively understanding the actions of others by putting yourself in their place to see the meaning they attach to social action, as well as what their goals are. This methodological approach to the question of how we can know things about the social world favours certain *qualitative* methods, such as observation, over others. An example may make this distinction clearer.

Consider the social setting within educational institutions known as the tutorial or class. If we started out wanting to know what happened within a particular tutorial setting, the two approaches outlined above would approach the question in different ways. Within the positivist tradition with its objectivist assumption, the preferred method for knowing what occurred within that setting would be to administer a questionnaire to participants on their perceptions of what was occurring. A sociologist operating within a qualitative, non-positivist tradition would probably seek to know what was occurring by sitting in the tutorial, observing the nature of the interaction and then interpretively understanding the meaning of what they saw (students nodding off, etc.). Each sociologist would seek to understand, but would do their Sociology in a different way. Both are legitimate ways of doing research but they are based on different epistemological traditions. In other words, the method chosen to investigate a subject arises out of a particular perspective.

The link between the perspective taken and the method used to gather data about the social world is clearly an important one. In terms of the particular perspectives of functionalism, conflict theory, and interactionism outlined above, the more structuralist accounts of functionalism and conflict theory tend, broadly speaking, to operate within a positivist tradition, while the interactionist perspective clearly operates within a non-positivist tradition using the methodology of *verstehen*.

Complementing the various assumptions, perspectives, and theoretical orientations of Sociology is the collection and use of empirical evidence or data. Data and methods have been mentioned a few times above as important components of the sociological imagination and the sociological quest. In the remainder of this chapter, we want to explore in greater detail the methods and uses of data in Sociology, thereby more fully answering the question of '*How can we know the social world?*'

Empirical evidence is generally referred to as data. *Data* is originally a Latin term meaning what can be seen or observed, and the original meaning is still applicable today. Data is collected through various methods such as a questionnaire, interview, observation, or a combination of these. Data has an intimate relationship to theory in building sociological knowledge, in that a theory is really only an opinion until it is supported with data that lends evidence to, or does not support, a theory. A major part of the attraction of Sociology is that some sociological theories resonate personally with us because they seem to provide explanations about how society works and our own experiences of it. At times some sociological theories take on the emotional and moral tenor of religious doctrine. Marxist theory, for instance, has this tendency for some, leading to a strongly held ideological position of Marxism. However, no matter how alluring or compelling a theory may seem, any theory that contributes to knowledge should be supported by empirical evidence for it to be considered a valid explanation of social phenomena.

A similar caveat applies to empirical evidence. Extolling research findings without an informed context or plausible explanation is called blind empiricism, and much confusion ensues when data is presented without context or theoretical grounding. Having a bunch of statistics or interview data fails to properly inform a situation or mean much until theory can provide a context and explanation for the patterns revealed by the data. Further, data's usefulness is also judged by its quality. Data quality is a product of the methodology associated with it. Shonky data, or data that we would more formally suggest is invalid and unreliable, is a product of poorly devised and executed methodology, essentially not measuring what it's supposed to, being unrelated to a theory, and ultimately not contributing to answering a research question.

The relationship between theory and empirical evidence is an intimate one then. Empirical evidence is used to test, revise, or build theory. While empirical evidence improves our understanding and is crucial to Sociology being a relevant perspective on the social world, it's also important to be aware that theory and evidence doesn't necessarily produce truth or immutable laws as earlier discussions about perspectives or approaches such as positivism outlined. At best, in sociology, we aim to gain greater clarity around the complexities of the social world and the experience of individuals and groups in it with the use of evidence and theory, but we cannot necessarily claim any such certainty as a social law or absolute truth.

In Sociology two approaches to the relationship between theory and data are apparent, informing various perspectives: inductive and deductive. An inductive approach commences with data that describe social patterns which are then lent interpretation and explanation with theory. Research that proceeds deductively, on the other hand, commences with a theory and collects data to test that theory. Many studies in Sociology are, in truth, a bit of both, given that research is very rarely entirely original. A classic work of inductive research in Sociology is Max Weber's famous study *The Protestant Ethic and the Spirit of Capitalism* (2002), in which Weber begins with a statement of his sociological problem through an analysis of some statistical patterns about the occupational status of Germany's Catholic and Protestant populations in the early years of the twentieth century. The regularities in the data, pertinent to specific cultural groups, describe a social pattern, but in and of themselves the data doesn't mean much beyond the plain statistical differences reported. The remainder of Weber's work is concerned with the development of a theory that employs both the historical and cultural sensibilities we encountered earlier, to explain why it is that Catholics and Protestants occupied starkly different positions within the German economy of that time.

Examples of deductive sociological research are the various attempts at replicating Pierre Bourdieu's *Distinction: a Social Critique of the Judgement of Taste* (Bourdieu 1984 [1979]). Bourdieu's famous work, which we encountered earlier, on the cultural tastes of the French in the late 1960s and early 1970s, used a survey to gather data to test the theory that cultural consumption was strongly influenced by social class and status. The survey data revealed numerous social patterns supporting Bourdieu's theory, such as the exclusive preference for classical music, serious novels, and fine art among the higher educated, wealthier, and high-status Parisian elite (more colloquially labelled as *high-brow snobs!*). Non-French replications inspired by his work (Bennett et al. 1999; 2008) commence with his theory of cultural capital as strongly influenced by social class and use both quantitative and qualitative data to test the theory in other national contexts. Some interesting variations and challenges to Bourdieu's ideas have ensued as the data from other countries reveal patterns such as the cultural omnivore (Peterson and Kern 1996) and the moral cultural consumer (Aarons 2021a), where musical taste is more eclectic or subject to certain cultural boundaries. Both Weber's and Bourdieu's work have led to ongoing research into questions about the relationship between religion and economic behaviour, and social class and culture. Replications of both Weber's and Bourdieu's work in different times and in different places have found similar but sometimes very different results, leading to interesting debates and theoretical refinements. In addition to being an example of how sociological practice entails the relationship between theory and data, this is how sociological knowledge is reflexive and follows the research process (see below).

A key concern with evidence represented by data and the quality of data is measurement, but measurement of what? Any statistic or text used in a sociological study is a measure of something. In empirical sociological research we aim to measure concepts. Concepts are related to theories. Theories are composed of propositions, and central to propositions are concepts. It is these concepts that Sociologists seek to measure when collecting data. Concepts relate to other concepts within a theory that explain social processes and formulate explanations for social phenomena. Data collection and data analysis aims to produce empirical results that support a theory or not through attempting to measure its components accurately, or what we call validly and reliably. For example, Sociologists interested in the impact of social class on health will need to collect data on both concepts through the development of measures of health and of social class but how do you define both concepts in order to measure them? What does 'health' mean and what is 'social class'? Further, if you were interested in collecting data on populism (the concept describing a certain style of politics we saw earlier) how would you define it and what questions about it would you pose to collect data about it? Similarly, Sociologists have faced challenges in defining other key concepts such as cosmopolitanism, religion, and poverty.

Empirical sociological research commonly employs two broad types of data: qualitative data and quantitative data. Qualitative data is textual, while quantitative data, as the name implies, is numeric. The organisation of theory and data in sociological research proceeds formally through a sequence of logical steps called the research process. When considering what data we need to collect and analyse, it's important to appreciate that in addition to the perspective a sociologist works in, approaches to data collection and data types relate directly to question types. The kind of data required in empirical research depends on what we want to find out. At times empirical approaches to research questions can be like the allure of some theories, with some researchers fiercely quantitative, and others routinely dismissive of quantitative approaches. While many Sociologists will prefer and develop expertise usually in one form of data collection and analysis, a good sociologist should appreciate the various uses, advantages, and limitations of any method and data. To restate then, a research method or means of collecting data is always decided by which kind of data is most appropriate to the research question. Qualitative data often best informs research that seeks to understand the experience, meaning, and feelings associated with a specific area of social life, as interpretive terms such as *verstehen* relate, while quantitative data is more appropriate to answering questions about broad patterns for large groups, sub-groups, and populations. Often sociological research combines both types of data, which complement one another very well, in mixed methods research or what's known as triangulation.

Qualitative data

Qualitative data are the varieties of textual evidence that a researcher collects through a range of methods used to answer questions that seek to understand the experience, meanings, and feelings of social phenomena. Most empirical research that employs qualitative data draws on interview data. Methods such as structured or semi-structured interviews or focus groups proceed with the researcher asking a series of questions of an interviewee or respondent whose answers form a bank of text, which is then organised under various themes related to a theoretical framework and various relevant concepts within it. Interviews are mostly one on one, with a researcher and a respondent; focus groups are generally composed of small groups of around 6–10 people. An interview typically takes around an hour, in which the researcher can ask a number of relevant questions around key concepts and themes. Focus groups are similar but, as the name implies, the questioning and discussion is focused on only a few key points about an experience or issue.

Beyond word-based text such as interview data, qualitative research often uses methods of data collection to include observations, sounds, and images. The social world is intricate and complex and there are various ways of 'reading' social interaction without necessarily asking people questions directly. For example, commercial advertising, media, and social rituals can be treated as 'texts' constituting data and analysed to discern patterns and then theorised. When we see an advertisement for a watch, a pair of shoes, or a car, what are the social messages that the advertisement is communicating, and why do advertisers aim to communicate in the ways they do? Of course, there is the explicit aim of selling you something, but how? Advertisements often contain representations and images of types of people, social roles, specific settings, and certain aesthetics; they conjure different forms of social desire in various ways that can suggest that when you purchase a particular product you are aligning yourself with a particular social or status group. Images and sounds (such as speech) are socially coded according to some Sociologists: unlocking and making known these codes enables researchers to learn about social interaction, socialisation, and how society is reproduced.

Another common form of collecting qualitative data is called ethnography. An ethnography can be a method and the end product of research such as a book or report. Typically, ethnography is based on observation or what's known as participant observation, where a sociologist is a part of the group or lives in close quarters to the group of interest. Qualitative data from observation are derived from field notes and are written up in forms such as rich description where a researcher details precisely a context, the various forms of behaviour of members of the group, the settings, and outcomes of interaction. While qualitative data is excellent for understanding the deeper meanings and social contexts of interaction, a limitation of this kind of evidence is that it cannot be used to claim a broad pattern that may be generalisable to a larger population.

Quantitative data

Quantitative data are numbers and statistics. Given that most Sociology students are in an Arts or related degree, the very mention of the 'S' word can have a highly adverse effect, turning would-be Sociologists away from key skills and access to large swathes of sociological research that use them. However, quantitative data and their uses need not be overly mathematically complex for them to be highly meaningful and very useful as evidence. There is perhaps an illusion that qualitative work is somehow easier than quantitative because of a lack of numbers (as suggested by such terms as 'hard' and 'soft' science/evidence), but qualitative data can be highly complex and difficult to interpret, so the notion of 'soft' is quite inadequate.

Quantitative data is best for approaching sociological problems that involve broad patterns for large groups, such as a community, sub-culture, nation or organisation. This kind of data allows the researchers to examine how various attributes, experiences, and identities are related to states, values, and opinions at the level of the individual, household, or larger group. Examples include the length of marriages and the impact of social class on divorce for some countries reported earlier, or how attitudes towards social issues such as immigration are defined by social groups categorised, for example, by age, education, or political affiliation, and further, how illnesses (such as COVID-19) are distributed in a country across various social groups. Relatedly, an advantage of quantitative data is that, if representative of a population through a good sample it can give accurate estimates and statistics for the whole population, unlike qualitative studies that focus only on a very limited number of cases. This makes quantitative methods and skills essential for various kinds of public decision making, such as social or public policy, giving Sociology graduates numerous vocational options (discussed in more depth in the next chapter).

Quantitative data is overwhelmingly collected through questionnaires (Aarons 2021b) but also via other modes such as content analysis, administrative data (such as police and health records), and observation. As we've seen, any statistic used in

Sociology is a measure of something, so quantitative methods are grounded in sociological theories by two important conditions: validity and reliability. The collection and analysis of quantitative data relies very much on careful planning and deliberation. Statistics are the end product of a series of questions that are designed to measure key concepts embedded within sociological theories. Concepts, however, are not always easily defined and a great deal of work is expended on how to define and operationalise concepts in sociological theories so as to best measure them. For example, some concepts might be quite uncomplicated such as age, life expectancy, or educational attainment, making them relatively easy to measure and collect data for, while others, as you will recall from the discussion earlier, are highly complex, such as health, poverty, cosmopolitanism, and cultural capital. The key to collecting valid and reliable quantitative data is having a clear definition of a concept and asking clear, non-ambiguous and non-judgemental questions in a questionnaire.

The research process

In the final section of this chapter, we briefly outline the research process. The research process can be seen as a more formal set of statements related to the five basic questions we encountered earlier:

1. What's happening? → Topic and research questions
2. Why? → Literature review
3. What are the consequences? → Theoretical framework
4. How do you know? → Empirical evidence: quant or qual data
5. How could it be otherwise? → Discussion, conclusion, and future options

How Sociologists conceive, design, and execute research, especially empirical research is subject to the research process. The research process is composed of a series of related and logical steps about refining a topic, crafting specific research questions, relating the project to the previous literature, contextualising and explaining the research within a theoretical framework, selecting an appropriate methodology, collecting and analysing data, and relating the findings and conclusions back to the general field. Any sociological research follows this process, yet the process can be iterative in that various steps can be reviewed and refined as the research progresses.

Conclusion

This chapter has considered the key relational components in building sociological knowledge. The question of '*How do we know?*' in Sociology is composed of perspectives, theories, and evidence. We have seen how sociological research proceeds formally through the research process and have examined the crucial relationship between theory and data as central to this process. This chapter has also explored in some detail different types of data and how empirical evidence is collected and used in sociological research. It was suggested that the collection and use of qualitative and quantitative data are appropriate to specific question types. Finally, there are limits to what we can know. As Sociology is a social science concerned with social behaviour and social patterns that are reproduced at some levels but change radically elsewhere, the question of 'how do we know?' implies no claim to absolute truth or social laws, but the discovery of social patterns and social meanings within the specific contexts of times and places.

References

Aarons, H., 2021a. 'Moral Distinction: Religion, Musical Taste, and the Moral Cultural Consumer', *Journal of Consumer Culture*, 21:2, 296–316.

—— 2021b. *A Practical Introduction to Survey Design: a Beginner's Guide*. Sage, London.

Bennett,T.,Emmison,M.,and Frow,J.,1999. *Accounting for Tastes:Australian Everyday Cultures*. Cambridge University Press, Sydney.

Bennett, T., Savage, M., Silva, E.,Warde, A., Gayo-Cal, M., and Wright, D., 2008. *Culture, Class, Distinction*. Routledge, London.

How do we know? 159

Bourdieu, P., 1984 [1979]. *Distinction: a Social Critique of the Judgement of Taste*. Routledge & Kegan Paul, London.
Peterson, R., and Kern, R., 1996. 'Changing Highbrow Taste: From Snob to Omnivore', *American Sociological Review*, 61:5 (October), 900–907.
Weber, M., 2002. *The Protestant Ethic and The Spirit of Capitalism*. Penguin Books, Harmondsworth.

9 Doing Sociology (and getting paid for it)

Careers and applications

In this final chapter we want to make a case for Sociology as an academic discipline with a set of skills that has a range of excellent applications for future careers. In many introductory Sociology texts and courses, not enough consideration is given over to just how relevant Sociology is to a variety of jobs. In response to any possible notion that Sociology is simply an academic discipline confined to the Ivory Tower whose rewards are navel gazing, and a sense of 'interesting but not very useful', we wish to inform you that Sociology is indeed practised in many places outside of the university. We'd also like to assure you that qualifications in Sociology with research skills through training in research methods can present you with a variety of job prospects and a means to make a positive difference to society. This chapter, then, can be thought of as an invitation to sociological practice, practice that is focused on being a sociologist outside of the university.

It is a fair and valid assumption that in addition to an 'interested for interest's sake' attitude towards study, many students these days are concerned about career prospects and will choose subjects at university that will have some vocational pay-off once they graduate. While we have made the case throughout the text that Sociology is a discipline that affords a unique perspective on human behaviour, you may be wondering well, I like the idea of Sociology as a meaningful discipline for understanding society,

DOI: 10.4324/9781003316329-9

but can it land me a job? The answer is most assuredly YES. In this chapter, we want to stress that in addition to identifying what is unique about Sociology in understanding social life, this knowledge is also highly applicable to various industry settings in an increasingly competitive job market. A further point about promoting Sociology as a discipline that equips you for a rewarding career is that, beyond any understandable personal ambition, applying the sociological perspective through research can actually help people work towards improving society for those that need it most. So, if you are interested in people, social change, confronting social problems, and making a difference, Sociology is a discipline that can be applied successfully to a range of industries and professions.

Given the scope and breadth of sociological theorising and range of methodological skills employed by Sociologists, it's no wonder that Auguste Comte (who gave the discipline its name as you'll recall) described Sociology as the 'Queen of the Social Sciences' (British Sociological Association n.d.). A cursory list of topics in sociological research should alert you to a range of career possibilities that Sociology can offer because they relate to the many common social issues and problems that governments and agencies are involved in trying to alleviate and solve. For example, key issues reflecting social inequality such as poverty, housing, transport, health, family functioning, racial equality and justice, and gendered disadvantage are fundamental concerns to any community. A key advantage of Sociology here is that the discipline has developed a long tradition of understanding – through theory and research – the various social causes and contexts of how these problems arise and what to do about them. Work in this field is mostly aimed at working with community or population level problems. John Goldthorpe (2016) has suggested that Sociology can be thought of as a 'population science', but one that is more focused on the supra-individual contexts of people and social patterns than say demography or statistics, and therefore a natural fit with many forms of working with people through public policy.

Accreditation and recognition

Unlike some other professions whose work is with and about people, Sociologists are not currently formally accredited by a peak body or governmental authority, as uniquely qualified for a specific vocation. A sociologist is 'accredited' through their degree qualification. Despite this, many employers recognise the skills and knowledge of Sociology graduates as highly suited to many positions, so accreditation is not necessary. To some extent such 'credentialism' is – as many Sociologists themselves have pointed out – not necessarily about the level of training and skills, but a means of guarding and inflating conditions around entry to a profession to ensure greater privileges for those already in it, such as higher pay and more autonomy. Formal recognition such as accreditation, while certainly necessary in some ways, may not always reflect quality and expertise. However, formal application of sociological approaches to social problems is gaining some ground. In some quarters there is a call for a more clinical version of Sociology (Rebach and Bruhn 2001). Clinical Sociology applies the sociological perspective to specific social problems within various contexts and designs interventions and policy options as significant responses to these problems. Clinical Sociology is also known as applied Sociology, or Sociology in action. A key example of applied Sociology is health policy and programmes derived from the insights of the social determinants of health, where health and illness rates are patterned by various social factors such as gender, socio-economic status, and ethnicity.

Value adding

While Sociology in and of itself can open-up many different career opportunities, certain interests and specific professions may require further specialised study. In this case, you can value add to a Sociology major knowing that you have a set of recognised skills related to a field of interest. If you are not a Sociology graduate or major, you may choose Sociology to strategically enhance career prospects to compliment other disciplines while working towards a qualification in a related field. For example, as noted above, many students interested in working with people or groups require specialised training and accreditation in a specific field such as Social Work or Psychology. Sociology is often a requirement for these qualifications and at the very least provides these formal qualifications with a deeper background knowledge of various social contexts within which client experience and professional practice takes place. Marketing is a similar discipline that requires a degree course or similar qualifications, yet an important criterion of being successful in marketing is an understanding of social patterns and social groups that relate to various forms of consumption. Further, courses in commerce and business utilise Sociology as ways of understanding work culture through disciplines such as organisational behaviour and human resource management or what are now – in an attempt to treat people as more than mere factors of production – termed, departments of 'people and culture'. Value adding to a Sociology major or another major through Sociology can take a number of forms. An increasingly important form of value adding is gaining further research skills through more advanced training in research methods. In addition to being able to collect and analyse qualitative data, intermediate and advanced quantitative related research skills such as statistics and data analysis, survey design, and the use of software for data analysis greatly enhance a graduate's capability.

Below are a number of key areas that routinely employ Sociologists. Many of these areas overlap and are interconnected, but within them are numerous specialisations and forms of practice that you should consider as potential career fields. Sociologists can work across these fields as practitioners or planners using the various kinds of fieldwork to conduct research or planning and administration of services and programmes. Further into a career, Sociologists often act as senior administrators and occupy leadership roles within relevant organisations.

Welfare and humanitarian work

Recall the idea presented earlier that the sociological quest entails sociological problems and social problems. We can put this into the form of a mantra: *all social problems are sociological problems, but not all sociological problems are social problems!* The fact that all social problems are also sociological problems suggests that much of the labour associated with welfare and humanitarian work involves a sociological perspective at some level. Welfare and humanitarian work cover a vast array of industries and jobs, social work being the most well-known, yet sociological knowledge and skills are relevant to almost all of them. Let's narrow this down to forms of community service and humanitarian work that will give you a clearer idea of how Sociologists contribute. Welfare and humanitarian agencies often arise to address particular needs for specific social groups – for example, agencies that provide services for victims of domestic violence, migrant youth, and economically disadvantaged families. Many of these agencies, in addition to being service providers, are also public advocates of the various groups that they serve and work hard to raise awareness of the issues that produce the forms of marginalisation which their clients experience; this often involves sociological research, policy analysis, and data collection and analysis. The research dimension of these service agencies is often based on sociological frameworks that inform service provision, programme design, and evaluation.

Public policy or social policy

Perhaps the most relevant and visible application of sociological knowledge and skills is in the realm of public or social policy. The various forms of planning and programmes for populations that issue from government as public or social policy are characterised by groups, institutions, and systems with specific aims and goals in mind. Public and social policy is designed and implemented at all levels of government, so a tremendous range of opportunities exist for a sociologist. Public policy is often derived from, or is a refinement of, sociological research – political ideology notwithstanding. Not all of it will be strictly sociological, but much of it will be, or will be related to key concepts in Sociology. Public policy research relies heavily on social research skills and the ability to collect and analyse both quantitative and qualitative data. Key areas of public or social policy include health, youth services, families, community services, and employment.

Private industry

While the range of sociologically relevant work in government and the public sector is extensive and perhaps intuitive, it may be a surprise to learn that many Sociologists are also suited to a range of professions in private industry.

Marketing

As stated above, marketing is an area that is perhaps not intuitively an obvious site for a sociologist to ply their skills; however, marketing is, in practice, a highly sociological field because marketers address the needs of their clients by working with consumers through analysis of social patterns and how products might be pitched to intended groups. While the jargon of marketing isn't necessarily the same as Sociology, the knowledge of social processes, group influences, socialisation through various agents, and the use of some sociological theories help marketers profile groups for markets or segments to promote consumption. Understanding of consumer practices therefore relies heavily on a sociological understanding of behaviour for individuals on the basis of membership of groups and households, albeit as units of consumption. Further, marketing is an intensely data rich industry. Marketers routinely collect and analyse various forms of quantitative and qualitative data about social groups and apply empirical insights to various campaigns targeting specific needs and wants. Marketing is as diverse as any field so there are some aspects of marketing that are a crucial public good, such as public health campaigns. However, marketing isn't always ethical, exploiting the experience of particular social problems and vulnerable groups in the name of sales, so perhaps the more Sociologists who become marketers will help improve its reputation!

Human resources

Human resources is about the ways in which organisations and companies manage their staff. Again, it's about people, and very much about culture, within an industrial or economic system and specific social context. A workplace has a range of concerns that are associated with harmonious and efficiently functioning operations that revolve around human behaviour in a group environment. A short list would include workplace policy development and implementation, relations between staff within an organisational hierarchy, identifying the source and working towards the alleviation of conflict between staff, recruitment and retention, and workplace stress and illness. All of these concerns involve various group-based forms of identity such as social class, gender, ethnicity, and status. Human resources specialists need to be aware of the various legal frameworks that govern workplace conduct and conditions, and a significant portion of work in this field is about complying with the law; however human resources departments are increasingly asked to think of ways of measuring and reflecting on staff climates within organisations to address the issues listed above.

Two examples will show how important a sociological perspective is to human resources. Firstly, workers and management can often be in conflict over wages and conditions, leading to industrial action, staff absenteeism, and high staff turnover. The conflict tradition in Sociology has a long history of tracing the systemic organisational causes of such disputes. Another increasingly important area of workplace functioning is gender and gender roles. The protracted efforts of women to gain access to the various professions, the experience of exploitation, balancing parenting and career progression, and the difficult ascent to leadership roles are all key areas relating how gender impacts the experience of work, within overt and covert patriarchal systems that encourage and reward men over women. Haydn was once involved in a study for a state government whose human resources department wondered why it could not recruit and retain female graduates. The government's own survey data showed very clearly that many young women left government roles within two years of commencing due to various forms of sexism and sexual harassment. Very high levels of dissatisfaction were correlated with the fact that the great majority of senior managers within the government's departments were older men.

Social impact research and evaluation

Many companies in private and public industry employ Sociologists in social impact and evaluation work. When a company wants to commence a project, such as the construction of major infrastructure or open a mine, that will cause some significant change to the living circumstances of an incumbent population, social, environmental, and economic impact assessments are often required by law. These assessments aim to measure positive and negative impacts or consequences of the planned project and assist in advising whether the project, or aspects of it, should be revised or changed, how, and to what extent. Social impact researchers and evaluators can even suggest that a project be not undertaken. Social impact can include the number of jobs a project may bring to a community or region, the impact on property and housing, transport, schooling, health, and disruption or enhancement of general living conditions. These kinds of evaluations are undertaken using a range of social research methods that collect both quantitative and qualitative data for individuals, households, and the community as a whole.

Evaluation research is also fundamental to government or agency programmes to measure the efficacy and effectiveness of various policy implementations that aim to address particular social or community problems. Without evaluation an agency has no way of knowing how effective or ineffective a policy is. Public funding and public support are often contingent upon empirical evidence that can state something accurate about the policy or programme. The importance of sociological skills here is shared with the previous section on public policy. Evaluators of social policy programmes require knowledge of particular groups, social contexts, supra-individual causes of problems encountered by individuals, and what the positive alternatives can be. Evaluation is usually performed by measuring some experience before and after a particular intervening action. For example, many governments are currently considering and trialling various forms of income support such as a universal basic income. For evaluators, there are questions such as what are the consequences of this kind of programme? Does universal basic income reduce poverty, increase family functioning, and alleviate poverty related social issues such as deaths of despair (Case and Deaton 2020)?

Journalism and private research companies

Much social research has an eager and invested public audience, and numerous publications and broadcasts outside of academia deliberate and comment widely on a variety of social issues. Most of the quality newspapers have social issues sections that draw on sociological research and sociological theories and are comprised of journalists and editors who have sociological training (or should). A feature that a Sociology graduate should have as a journalist is some level of expertise on the use of data in social issues, especially social statistics, but also the many nuances of qualitative data. Good journalism often requires the clear and effective communication of complex ideas to a non-expert public; having a Sociology major equips a journalist to communicate complex social issues and problems based in the social contexts relevant to the issue. In addition to journalism and broadcasting, Sociologists are also employed in private research companies such as Pew Research, and polling companies that produce various research reports on public opinion.

Higher degrees and further training

Naturally, in addition to the range of vocational prospects available for Sociology graduates, further study can enable greater access to further career possibilities. Honours, Masters, and PhD programmes all build on key knowledge and skills in Sociology and can be applied to specific fields that are directly related to the various vocational fields discussed above.

Enhancing a CV, and internships and work placements

An excellent way of enhancing your employment prospects is through an internship or work placement. Skills in Sociology are well recognised in many industries, allowing students to apply for a wide range of internships and work placements. However, it may not be obvious to you how you might find or apply for a work placement or internship, or how your studies in Sociology are relevant to these opportunities. There is a range of literature that assists you in sourcing and applying for internships, and jobs, as well as some useful websites, but a good guide specifically related to Sociology is Jackie Carter's (2021) *Work Placements, Internships and Applied Social Research*.

An important aspect of gaining entry to relevant employment or an internship, of course, is a well-developed and effective resume or CV. This should state the Sociology subjects you have completed but can be strategically expanded upon to include the specific knowledge, skills, and experiences gained from them that are relevant to the position. For example, many majors in Sociology require students to take research methods units to gain skills in the collection and analysis of qualitative and quantitative data, which are very attractive to employers. The skills and examples from these units can be separated out and listed, presenting a clear and attractive suite of highly relevant skills to many positions associated with the fields we have discussed above. Further, brief descriptions of work done in these units, such as research reports using data, can be recorded as examples of the application of these skills. The two examples below are only suggestions.

Quantitative skills

- Survey design – knowledge of key components in the survey design process, questionnaire design, and survey administration.
- Sampling techniques – knowledge of how to construct a basic random sample.
- Data analysis – high level of competency in data analysis software packages: SPSS, Stata, Microsoft Excel, R, etc.
- Basic statistics – univariate and bivariate analyses of large-scale national data using SPSS, Stata, Microsoft Excel, R, etc.
- Data visualisation – effective use of data analysis software to produce highly effective visualisation of data.

How I used these skills

My major research assignment empirically investigated important patterns in the social determinants of health to assess the impacts of gender, social class, ethnicity, and geography, on four key areas of health and illness. To do this I used national population health data, identifying and operationalising four key independent variables and four dependent variables. I analysed the data using univariate statistics to assess health and illness for the general sample, and bivariate analyses to investigate the impact the different social factors had on the distribution of illnesses reported in the survey. Findings were presented in tables and charts and suggested that health and illness is strongly correlated with all of the social factors assessed.

Qualitative skills

*   Research design – identifying appropriate research method, thematic discussion, contextualised within extant literature.
*   Interview question development – structured and semi-structured interview development for individual respondents and a focus group.
*   Respondent recruiting – promotion of my study via social media, filtering appropriate respondents.
*   Data collection – conduct of interviews and a focus group, data recording via recording device and notes.
*   Data analysis – data transcription, and thematic analysis of interview data using NVIVO.

How I used these skills

My major research report investigated the meanings and narratives of challenges associated with student life during the pandemic through semi-structured interviews and a focus group. I collected data on the impact of casual work, mental health challenges, and student isolation on motivation to stay at university during the pandemic. The ten interviews produced rich descriptive data that revealed three consistent themes among respondents. Students spoke most of a deep sense of helplessness and anomie as a result of the pandemic, which had severely reduced their motivation for study. An unexpected finding was that many respondents had taken up creative outlets to deal with the negative impacts of the pandemic on study at university. The focus group asked respondents about the value of on-campus classes. Focus group data revealed three main themes that participants felt to be of crucial importance in studying on campus: solidarity, belonging, and access to resources. Responses and themes differed due to gender and social class.

Conclusion

This chapter has offered an invitation to sociological practice, principally outside of the university. As students are naturally interested in how a discipline with its knowledge and skills might enhance career prospects, this chapter offers insight into the various industries and occupations within which many Sociology graduates have found rewarding careers. In complex global societies, as key knowledge and skills in the determinants of individual lives through social processes, social systems, and institutional impacts becomes increasingly important, the vocational relevance of sociological knowledge and research skills will only increase.

References

British Sociological Association, n.d. 'Speak_up_for_Sociology_leaflet. pdf', britsoc.co.uk.

Carter, J., 2021. *Work Placements, Internships & Applied Social Research.* Sage, London.

Case, A., and Deaton, A., 2020. *Deaths of Despair and the Future of Capitalism.* Princeton University Press, Princeton.

Goldthorpe, J., 2016. *Sociology as a Population Science.* Cambridge University Press, Cambridge.

Rebach, H., and Bruhn, J. (eds), 2001. *Handbook of Clinical Sociology*, 2nd edn. Springer, New York.

Index

For Product Safety Concerns and Information please contact our EU
representative GPSR@taylorandfrancis.com
Taylor & Francis Verlag GmbH, Kaufingerstraße 24, 80331 München, Germany

www.ingramcontent.com/pod-product-compliance
Lightning Source LLC
Chambersburg PA
CBHW052008270326
41929CB00015B/2834